MONASTERE
NOTRE-DAME
de
L'ATLAS

D1025609

Midelt. The town lies in the geographic center of Morocco, approximately two hundred kilometers south of Fès, along the mountainside of the Atlas Mountains. A community of four Trappist monks lives here.

They called their monastery "Our Dear Lady of Atlas," exactly as the previous monastery of Tibhirine was called, in which one of them once lived. [above]

Brother Jean-Pierre Schumacher is the last survivor of a massacre that stunned the world. [below]

Jean-Pierre thinks of the seven murdered brothers every day. It is his special concern that they are not forgotten. For that reason he tells his and their story in this book—a story full of love for God and mankind.

Jean-Pierre dressed in his Trappist habit in the cloister of the monastery.

THE LAST MONK
of TIBHIRINE

THE LAST MONK
of TIBHIRINE

*A True Story
of Martyrdom,
Faith,
and Survival*

❖

FREDDY DERWAHL

WITH PHOTOGRAPHS BY BRUNO ZANZOTERRA
TRANSLATED BY ANDREAS KIRYAKAKIS AND RUTH I. CAPE

PARACLETE PRESS
BREWSTER, MASSACHUSETTS

2013 First printing

The Last Monk of Tibhirine: A True Story of Martyrdom, Faith, and Survival

English translation copyright © 2013 by Paraclete Press, Inc.

ISBN 978-1-61261-374-1

Original title: *Der letzte Mönch von Tibhirine* by Freddy Derwahl © 2012 by adeo Verlag in der Gerth Medien GmbH, Asslar, a division of Verlagsgruppe Random House GmbH, München, Germany.

Scripture quotations are taken from The New Jerusalem Bible, published and copyright © 1985 by Darton, Longman & Todd Ltd and Les Editions du Cerf, and used by permission of the publishers.

Photographs copyright © Bruno Zanzoterra

The Paraclete Press name and logo (dove on cross) is a trademark of Paraclete Press, Inc.

Library of Congress Cataloging-in-Publication Data

Derwahl, Freddy, 1946-
  [Letzte Mönch von Tibhirine. English]
  The last monk of Tibhirine : a true story of martyrdom, faith, and survival / Freddy Derwahl ; with Photographs by Bruno Zanzoterra ; Translated by Andreas Kiryakakis and Ruth Cape.
      pages cm
  Summary: "The Last Monk of Tibhirine is the story of the Cirstercian monk Jean-Pierre Schumacher, the last surviving member of a monastic community which was kidnapped and killed in Algeria in 1996"— Provided by publisher.
  Includes bibliographical references and index.
  ISBN 978-1-61261-374-1 (pbk.)
  1. Schumacher, Jean-Pierre. 2. Trappists—Algeria—Tibehirine—Biography. 3. Christian martyrs—Algeria—Tibehirine—Biography. 4. Victims of terrorism—Algeria—Biography. 5. Notre Dame de l'Atlas (Monastery : Tibehirine, Algeria) I. Title.
  BX4705.S51398D4713 2013
  272'.909653–dc23   2013025886

10 9 8 7 6 5 4 3 2 1

All rights reserved. No portion of this book may be reproduced, stored in an electronic retrieval system, or transmitted in any form or by any means—electronic, mechanical, photocopy, recording, or any other—except for brief quotations in printed reviews, without the prior permission of the publisher.

Published by Paraclete Press
Brewster, Massachusetts
www.paracletepress.com

Printed in the United States of America

Dedicated to the monks of Midelt in gratitude

"One can trample down seven flowers, but one cannot prevent them from blossoming again in the spring."

(Entry by an unknown person in the book of condolences at the memorial celebration for the seven murdered monks in Paris, 1996)

CONTENTS

IN THE SHADOW
OF BLACK MOUNTAINS

T HERE IS A "TEA SALON" LOCATED IN ONE OF THE BACK
buildings of the Atlas monastery; however, "salon" merely
refers to the hastily painted word above the entrance.
In spite of this rather grand description, two rickety benches and
tables are sufficient to carry on a good conversation. A gas cooker
and cans filled with tea stand in a niche where twice a day, at 10:30
AM and 4:30 PM, a strong group of four French Trappist monks
and their Moroccan workers meets in this narrow room. Omar, a
fifty-six-year-old Muslim with fiery eyes, is in charge; he is responsible for the infusion of tea, pouring hot water into a dented pot
brimming with fresh peppermint. The aroma from the tea is the
best part about it since it creates a sense of pleasant anticipation.

I still have to familiarize myself with the inevitability of this
place. As the hour for the break chimes, Bara, a widowed sister-
in-law of Omar, rushes through the hallway of the inn, knocks
on the cell doors, and calls out, "Tea, tea!" as if somewhere a fire
had broken out. Everyone in the "salon" greets everyone else with
a handshake and wishes for a pleasant day or night, even if they
have met many times before. This is part of Muslim tradition and
strengthens solidarity. The sugary, hot drink is of excellent quality,

and savoring it limits conversation to a minimum. Here one uses first names, because everyone is in the same boat. The prior's wearing jeans and a T-shirt sets aside the rules of the "Cistercian Order of Strict Observance" for fifteen minutes and conforms to the customs of the Muslim neighbors. These are the small interreligious connections that break up the long daily routine, which for the monks lasts from the vigil around 4 AM to Compline at 9:00 PM.

Thus the tea breaks in this storage room are strongly symbolic of what happens here at the foot of the High Atlas on this solitary outpost of Christian monasticism: simple modesty, hearty friend-ship, and a hint of an attempt of a few courageous men to be more forward-thinking and ecumenical in the vast ocean of two world religions. When the Trappists and their assistants shake hands several times a day and wish each other "Salam-Peace," these are small gestures, but they mean much more than all other forms of official dialogue between them. They do not feel there is anything special about doing this, but know that only by taking small steps will relationships improve and deepen. One does not expect a medal for bravery, merely a bit of understanding.

The distance from the imperial city of Fès to our destination, the mountain city of Midelt, was two hundred kilometers. The drive led from the ancient sites of Islamic wisdom and scholarship out into the simple countryside. By contrast, the social landscape extends from the beautiful college student in tight jeans to the des-titute shepherds with their herds of sheep and goats searching for greenery among thistle flowers. A well-guarded imperial residence is located in Infran, where smoke from brown nomadic tents rises skyward. Here colorful clothes wave like the flags of Tibetan mountain farmers in the hot desert wind, and one encounters market towns like in the Wild West. Here and there one finds dense forests that have asserted themselves against cliffs and sand. Along sparse rivulets one notices children playing soccer in Barcelona uniforms, and along the country road one spots honey and fig sellers. For the most part, however, there are just great expanses and great loneliness, until suddenly in the middle of the midday heat an old, bearded man with his beast of burden emerges like an apparition from the middle of nowhere, prompting the questions: Where is he coming from, and where is he going?

From an eastward direction, the Atlas Mountains gradually rise and reach an elevation of 3,270 meters at Arachy. The silhouette of the mountain range still lies in fog, but around the area of Midelt it increasingly changes in color to a powerful blackness, like a wall. Behind it one can imagine the immensity of the Sahara desert and the gates leading into the Black Africa. Even though the interplay of light at this height changes several times a day and becomes snow-covered at the latest in late fall, I will call them the "Black Mountains" during the next few weeks. This color greatly stands out and gives a mythical quality to the transitions in the landscape. Through the window of the monastery cell I will constantly gaze at the mountain chain, continuously spellbound by a certain power, something that wants to elevate me to encounter the Sacred.

The city of Midelt is a gray, unobtrusive city whose heyday as the center of the iron ore industry lies in a distant past. In the shadow of the massive mountains, it now extends in all directions, with some 60,000 inhabitants living dispersed in the foothills of the promontories. A back road extends from the eastern edge of town to the monastery, where the outskirts of the town suddenly end at a high wall with a watchtower on both sides of the locked entrance gate. Behind it lies a gravel courtyard that resembles a barrack square. The windows have bars on them, and the afternoon silence is ominous. It makes me think of Tibhirine, the Algerian monastery, and the seven decapitated monks. Everything here is reminiscent of a defensive stronghold aimed at preventing another nighttime attack from unknown assailants. In spite of the fact that this military appearance is rather deceptive, with the architecture dating back to a former convent of Franciscan sisters, the name "Tibhirine" is present at every step.

In the Monastery of Our Lady of Atlas, opposite the portals, one finds a door with the inscription "Mémorial," and behind the door is a confined space with a commemorative room reminiscent of a funeral chapel, meant for all visitors who wish to show their respect for the seven martyrs of Tibhirine and to enter their own names into the memorial book. The picture of the Virgin Mary in the apse of the adjacent monastery chapel comes from the prayer room of the Algerian Trappists, and an icon in bright colors depicts the seven sleeping monks. Their photographs are on the walls of the guest wing. Besides works by Pope John Paul II and the Cistercian writer Guillaume of St. Thierry, thriving literature about the murdered monks is on display for reading. Finally, a poster reminds one of the movie *Of Gods and Men* by Xavier Beauvois, who made the film about the mystery of Tibhirine that generated worldwide attention. Once again, one can see them sit around the table of their small chapter hall in which the decisive meetings took place, and the decision was made not to give in to the threats of the "brothers from the mountains." "At night," the monks said, "they take up arms and we take up the book."

Even in my small three-by-three-meter simple cell I find memorial notes with the seven heads and a prayer of remembrance. A palm branch with a crown of Mary in a niche of the wall is the only evidence of any color; a miniature copy of the Jerusalem Bible lies on a corner table next to a small reading lamp. I brought along only three books: *Jesus of Nazareth* by Pope Benedict XVI (to keep up), *God Any Day* by Christian de Chergé, the murdered prior of Tibhirine (as an introduction to Christian-Islamic thought), as well as Ernst Jünger's *Seventy Gone* (a diary for stylistic exercises). Opposite a coatrack, there are a sink and a mirror, and next to a nightstand is a lovely hard bed. Outside the window there is a small flower garden with mallows, four-o'clock flowers (marvel of Peru), and cacti, and behind them the Black Mountain chain; it is a view that will suffice for weeks.

When Jean-Pierre appeared at the gate in the late afternoon of my arrival, we immediately embraced each other. He knew what I expected of him—namely, that I hoped he would relate the whole story to me. I found the slightly bent-over eighty-seven-year-old Trappist monk in good spirits. His blue-green eyes accentuated an impish smile that concealed great kindness. Deep wrinkles on his forehead and his chin did not bear the signs of worry but of wisdom. He wore a sand-colored habit typical for this climate, with a leather belt, and on his head a knit tarbush bearing Islamic motifs. I knew that his name was Schumacher, but I was not aware that he came from Luxemburg or that we had acquaintances in common from the Luxemburg-German-French border triangle along the Mosel River. This already gave us the impetus for our first conversation. The next morning at 10:30, we sat down together for the first time. Our only topic was his life. The massacre of his seven brothers lay fifteen years in the past. He, however, had been spared from the attack, so where had his fate led him since then?

At the Midelt monastery one belongs to a somewhat extended family where everyone uses first names, which is, of course, also true for the prior but causes some problems because both he and brother Flachaire have the same first name of Jean-Pierre, thus one calls one the "elder" and the other the "younger." In order to better distinguish between the two, this book will simply make the distinction between "prior" and "Jean-Pierre." I will abstain from abbreviations like F. (Father) and B. (Brother) because they do not fit within this circle of monastic friends. In this way the reader can more easily distinguish between the individuals.

Jean-Pierre and I had actually met at Tibhirine in 1987, some ten years before the abduction. He was a monk responsible for running errands that later became life-threatening, and I was an "observer," or as the Trappists used to say, "the new guy." It was the time of Ramadan, the Islamic month of fasting, and I still remember that at the break of dawn both of us used to spend some time in silence on the flat roof of the monastery. There was a gentle breeze and stars glimmered in the sky, while in the villages on the other side of the Atlas Mountains the inhabitants exuberantly celebrated the end of fasting. Back then Jean-Pierre caught my eye, because with his wide forehead, light hair, and his quiet demeanor he reminded me of my father.

Before the first Vespers in the chapel at Midelt, this attitude of Jean-Pierre once again caught my attention. The old man was kneeling on the ground, and later he read and sang with his glasses on the tip of his nose. Because of the heat the four monks did not wear the heavy white cowls. Here, a simply dressed group who recited psalms from the Old Testament was praying for the poor, injured, and seeking people in the world. The monastery is dedicated to our dear "Lady of Atlas" as it was also called in Tibhirine. The designation "Dear Lady" precedes every name of a Trappist monastery worldwide. Here, in the midst of Islam whose Qur'an also adores Mary, this truly holds a special meaning. It creates transitions whose quiet and binding nature lie so dear to the heart of the Christian guests in this country.

This closeness became especially palpable when at 8:30 in the evening, Compline, the night prayer, began. Here the old Gregorian chants of the Salve Regina, where one entrusts oneself to the "Mother of Mercy," blended in with the prayer calls of the muezzin sounding from the pointed towers of the mosques, suggesting that the quiet and loud do have a trace of commonality at their core.

The night is drawing near, the mountains are black, and in the treetops a strong wind rustles.

July 19, 2011

7:15 AM: Holy Mass. The Sanctus and Lord's Prayer are in Arabic, although no Muslim ever enters the chapel. A crucified God is inconceivable to them. But one understands it as a gesture, and even though not much is accomplished, one remains open-minded.

Jean-Pierre, with his stooped body at the choir, becomes as of today my counterpart, my partner, and I wish him to be my paternal friend. His eyes reflect only kindness, but they also suggest adventure and confrontation with death.

The high voices are those of the Franciscan sisters, who have lived here for decades and are all over eighty; they do not wear habits, and are modest, nameless heroines.

8:00 AM: Breakfast with Nunu, a thirty-four-year-old Spanish Friar Minor preparing for his eternal vows, who looks like the singer Julio Iglesias, only somewhat scrubbier. He has been working for five years in small communities in Granada, Seville, and Tangier, catering to the handicapped, aged, dying, and all those whom otherwise no one helps. After his conversation with Jean-Pierre, Nunu calls him "the pearl, the treasure in the field."

10:30 AM: After tea Jean-Pierre says, "*on y va*—let's go," which can also be understood as a question, but underneath it is something of that Cistercian discipline whose daily routine is strictly regulated by the chiming of the bells. He then unlocks the door to the "memorial," the small commemorative room for his seven brothers, who had died in the highland of Tibhirine as a result of having their throats cut.

On the floor is a seven-armed lamp stand and above it are the portraits of the murdered monks as well as of the survivor Amédée who, in the meantime, has passed away. On a podium lectern there is copy of the handwritten testament of Prior Christian that has attracted worldwide attention as a text directed at the "friend of my last minute." It is a shattering small tract.

Everything in the guest room where our daily meetings take place is very Moroccan, and I merely have to say a word and the old man begins to narrate.

12:30 PM: Our noon meal at the round guest table consists of zucchini soup, onion pancakes, and ice-cold water. The rule of silence is not taken too seriously. Prudi, a small robust Andalusian woman, talks about her experience converting from Islam to Christianity: the drama at Tibhirine had moved her deeply.

3:10 PM: The three hours allotted for the siesta is generous. The temperature reaches its height at 105.8 degrees F. My first encounter with Jean-Pierre was encouraging, and his life unfolds like a beautiful story. It feels strange to awaken from European dreams deep inside Morocco, dragging one's latent experiences all the way to the Atlas Mountain chain; Freud would be powerless. Bright light streams in as I open the curtain.

3:45 PM: Reading of Christ's agony at Gethsemane at None, the ninth hour, is the most difficult time of day, with the heat weighing heavily on the chapel, where a day can unexpectedly take a turn for the worse.

4:30 PM: Reading three DIN-A4 sized pages full of closely written notes I had taken during our conversations strengthens my conviction to become what I should be, namely an author who writes about a yearning for God, albeit to discover him through a descent into hell.

9:00 PM: A fresh wind blows through the pine trees. Immediately after Compline, the "Grand Silence" prescribed in the Rule of St. Benedict begins. There is still a trace of fiery-red sunlight above the mountains. The guard has locked all of the gates and now I am locked in, but I think that there are good reasons.

THE MILL IN BUDING

BUDING IS A VILLAGE IN THE BORDER TRIANGLE OF FRANCE, Luxembourg, and Germany. With a population of 488 people, it is too small to be called a township; however, seen through the eyes of a child, it is the whole world. Even at the age of eighty-seven, Jean-Pierre still has this childlike glow in his eyes and says about his home: "It was a land of dreams; it was a paradise." At the heart of this magnificence was a mill. It was a remote place located a few kilometers from the center of the village at the banks of the Canner River, a small tributary of the Mosel River, which people around there call "the Big Sister." The clear water made its way in a meandering pattern through the meadows to its mouth at Köningsmacker. A donkey trail connected the house with the country road going toward Elzing. Jean-Pierre's father had built a bridge at the end of the forest path in 1930, which was later blown up several times during the World War in order to halt the advance of the enemy.

An idyllic setting of forest, meadows, and fields provided the backdrop for pictures Jean-Pierre had taken in his younger days. They were lusterless pictures of an area that the inhabitants considered a sort of "Lorraine Switzerland." It is a declaration of a love that generously conceals that one had to work very hard in this part of the country. But it also continuously created close ties with suppliers and retailers in the area. In Letzeburg Low German one said in Buding, *"Ech gin and Millen"* (I've gone milling), and everyone, of course, knew what was meant. They all belonged to the Grand Duchy of Luxembourg, but one differentiated between a hardly noticeable preference for France and some opposition against militant Germany. One sang the national anthem, "We Remain What We Are," to which Jean-Pierre softly added, "We don't want to be Prussians."

Jean-Pierre Schweitzer, the grandfather on his mother's side, acquired the mill along with three water wheels and moved there with two horses and a covered wagon. Emil Schumacher, his father, expanded the mill and acquired five cows, two horses, chickens, and rabbits. One produced milk, butter, cream, bread, and cheese. In winter, the pigs were slaughtered for sausage, ham, and liver pate. If in the spring there was a flood, the mill came to a standstill between the two river branches, but the time was used to repair leather accessories for the animals or agricultural equipment. There were also a large vegetable garden and fruit trees, which assured that the family was self-sufficient and could live a life free of constraints. If there was ever need in the area, the father was always ready to help with provisions. In order to make deliveries to customers, a maid of orthodox origin, as well as a servant who helped the father, had to be employed. Both were treated like brother and sister by the family because to Jean-Pierre, solidarity with strangers was important; when they later disappeared in the confusion of the war, he took it very hard.

In those days there were fourteen mills in the Canner valley; many apprentices came there from Bavaria in order to learn the language. Luxembourg was considered a hospitable country, more so among the farmers and artisans than among the people in the cities. There was also an unquestioning willingness to help each other. If necessary, everyone pitched in.

Next to the large kitchen a water wheel provided for animal feed, another for cement, and a third one milled flour. The water—its scent and its sounds—to them was home. As to flour, the pious Schumacher family very early put it within a religious context. A testament to this is proclaimed in the following nightly psalm: "Yet in my heart thou hast put more happiness than they enjoyed when there was corn and wine in plenty." The father referred to the process of milling as "work for purification." Jean-Pierre's sister Marie-Therese, who had a disposition toward poetry, found appropriate passages in the Holy Scripture, which praised bread as a symbol of life "that always lasts and never ends."

Jean-Pierre, the eldest of five brothers and two sisters, was born on February 15, 1924. When one of his little brothers died at the age of eight months, the carpenter made a small casket, and the mother placed the dead son in it. The later monk has a vivid memory of this ritual, stating: "There appeared to be something monastic in our family. Sunday Mass was followed by Vespers in the afternoon, and major holidays were celebrated with much splendor. On Christmas, father decorated the Christmas tree, and at Easter, mother would color and hide the decorated eggs in the garden; at Saint Nicholas Day, we children would place a plate on the windowsill," and in February, there was a present for the birthday child Jean-Pierre.

It became apparent that the boys kept mostly to themselves and avoided contact with the parents. After Vespers they disappeared into the forest, whose dark beauty had always fascinated the eldest son of the Schumacher family. "Perhaps"—he smiled reflectively— "the history of my calling began on those paths."

Starting school meant an end to the carefree and playful days. The teacher was unusually strict, and the surprised pupil had to live with his grandfather, serve everyday as an altar boy in Mass, and memorize the catechism at his aunt's. During church service, the organist chanted a Gregorian chant. "Even today I still hear his voice," the one-time altar boy remembers, noting that he especially looked forward to Holy Week. In groups of three they had to go through the village and collect eggs from the blacksmith, baker, tailor, and the merchants, with one third of the latter being Jews; anyone who refused to make a donation had eggs thrown at his door.

The Jewish neighbors and that orthodox maid gave rise in Jean-Pierre to sensitivity for ecumenism without his having sought it. Yet it was still too early for such contemplations. Nevertheless, he well remembers that the maid attended Catholic Sunday Mass and also went to confession. The Jews also came to church for funerals and left again during the offerings, but his Jewish classmates did not participate in the same religious instruction. During the Feast of Tabernacles, the Jews entered the small synagogue carrying barkless palm branches; as a sign of redemption, they threw bread pieces into the river. However, when the Germans advanced into the area, they all disappeared and only the butcher's wife returned. When Jean-Pierre celebrated his first Mass, the Jewish woman left her house and came to the procession to congratulate him. Jean-Pierre says, "I loved this gesture."

The dark liturgy of Good Friday started at dawn with a full spring moon in the sky. The organist sang the lamentations of Jeremiah, and the altar boy was allowed to turn the clapper instead of the bells, because "the bells had flown to Rome," to the pope, and following the moving song, to extinguish the thirteen candles.

The Procession of the Feast of Corpus Christi was no less exciting. During the procession birch branches were carried along, and the houses and windows were decorated with flowers and pine branches. The girls were dressed in white like angels and walked before the Sacrament of the Altar while the firemen fought over the privilege to carry the "canopy of heaven." At the end, the priest quietly gave the benediction.

Jean-Pierre had a somewhat ambiguous relationship to this priest who, on account of the concordat, was allowed to teach Bible studies. Nevertheless, he remembers walking with him to the little lineman's house along the Coal and Steel Street between Saarland and Lorraine, where for the first time he saw a dying person receiving the last rites. This experience, the first encounter of a sensitive child with death, made an impression on him and played an important role in his later calling.

He often laughed about the church usher who was like a "policeman" during church service and with his spear tried to gain respect from the rowdy group of children and the silly altar boys wearing their red and white collars. Whoever disobeyed had to kneel down in the central knave as a punishment.

In this context Jean-Pierre remembers the *us et coutumes* (customs and traditions) of the Trappist abbeys before the Council, where the "sinner" after a "chapter of faults," like dropping a plate, had to lie down in the entryway to the dining room in self-accusation, until the whole community had walked over him. Still today it angers him that the worst punishment consisted in begging the monks on one's knees for food, which then had to be eaten on the floor of the refectory. Since the monks who ate with spoons and from plates were not allowed to order anything for themselves but only for their neighbors, a strange incident occurred one day: one of the Fathers found a mouse in his soup and complained in the required sign language that his two tablemates had not received a mouse.

In a small volume entitled *The Path of Our Childhood: The Place Called Buding's Mill,* published in 2004, Marie-Thérèse Schumacher wrote a moving tribute to the old hometown. It reveals much about the quiet joyfulness of the miller family that relied on its own merits and solidarity and was well respected in the surrounding villages. Here one gathered for the holidays while enjoying pastries and baked goods, and the festivities at the Canner River always lasted a good three days. The close ties of this community were also noticeable during the family gatherings that took place every Sunday. Monday was always a memorial day for the dead, which everyone celebrated with a Mass.

When asked whether he feared his parents, Jean-Pierre replies that they were both good, and strict, but that at times, he took cover from his father, whereas his mother, in her loving way, gave him everything that makes someone's childhood and youth enjoyable. During vacations, the family went to the Hohenfels area in Luxembourg, where an aunt treated everyone to her wild berry cakes, but where they also worked hard together in the wheat, beet, and potato fields since a lot of work had to be done.

It was a heavy blow for the family when his seventy-four-year-old father became seriously ill. His mother cared for him until he died. At that time, Jean-Pierre was already a monk in Algeria, but he was still able to see his father on his deathbed, and even today remembers his final words: "The Lord cares in a special way for the parents of a priest." His mother spent her old age in happiness; she had always been a strong woman and died at the age of eighty-nine, and it was her son who gave her the last blessing in her casket.

July 20, 2011

3:30 AM: The best invention in my cell is definitely the fly screen.

7:15 AM: Jean-Pierre reads the Mass that begins and ends with Lauds. Jubilation about creation, "You nations, clap your hands." The parable of the sower fits well into this barren landscape of mountain farmers and donkey carts. Jean-Pierre utters the words of the Eucharist and with his hands that are marked by manual work lifts up the Holy Host. Then he prays for the pope and the deceased; some of them he knows very well—he will never forget them.

8:10 AM: The Spanish Franciscan Nanu with his fiery eyes and long black hair still wet from the shower is kneeling on the floor during Mass. He will depart and states that his stay here was the "breakthrough" for him.

10:00 AM: I am seized by an illness that the prior calls "the tourist's illness." Even the Guest Father José-Luis smiles mentioning that intestinal cramps and diarrhea were pretty normal here; besides, he adds that the pain makes prayers much more "tangible." No visit to the tea salon or to lunch for me today; tonight he plans to bring me a bowl of rice.

3:00 PM: During our siesta a storm erupts, sending powerful gusts through the pine tree as if we were at high sea; the wind howls through the narrow halls of the monastery, and once in a while a door slams. The fluttering curtains reveal the glimpse of a blue, leaden, cloudless sky. Only the mountains lie in a fog as if they were the unshakable originator of this spectacle.

4:30 PM: During my search for information about Tibhirine, I find a sentence about it from one of Christian's letters, dated 1978. It reads: "I am a house of prayer, which is at the same time a den of thieves."

7:50 PM: While washing dishes Puri says that during spiritual retreats Jean-Pierre does not lecture her, but interprets Bible texts with her, and "he goes into depth."

8:00 PM: The prior has invited me to speak to the community in a room where the daily chapter meeting takes place. On the walls hang four large portraits of deceased Christian heroes and heroines from the Atlas Mountains, role models for dedication in a solitary environment. What should I tell them in this room that reminds me so much of Tibhirine and the tables where the big decision was made not to give in to the terror? I tell them of my trips and projects for novels, while the four listen in silence and no one asks a question. After a ten-minute delay, we leave the room one by one to attend Compline in the chapel.

11:00 PM: The wind has died down, and the dogs bark, something that I will have to get used to. There is no night rest for me, but the prior tells me that I could sleep here whenever I wished, except in the two hours in the morning when I meet with Jean-Pierre.

As I reflect on the men who sleep in this house, I realize they are serious, yet relaxed. Their encounter with women is uncomplicated—it's a kind of tender chasteness, where the monks are like older brothers putting their arms around one. There is nothing they have not endured. This is a completely different kind of Christianity than we encounter in the old Europe.

12:30 AM: These dogs are a real nuisance, and it is virtually impossible to sleep. I read the diary entries in *Seventy Gone* by Ernst Jünger, who does not disappoint me. Just while leafing through the pages, I already find eight references that also apply to the drama at Tibhirine, to persevering in the face of death.

WAR YEARS

URING THE NEW YEAR'S EVE CELEBRATION OF 1936, mother suddenly noticed that her oldest son was missing. When she entered his bedroom, she saw him lying on his bed in tears agonizing over an important decision that he had to make: whether he should remain at home and work in his father's mill or attend the college of Sierck-les-Bains. Yet his sadness had deeper roots, which were grounded in his desire to become a priest, a desire that had grown in Jean-Pierre ever since he was five years old. Everything in his childhood had led him in that direction: his pious parental home, his closeness to the parish, the influence of the priests and teachers, and nature around him. In an emotional outburst to his mother, he confided to her his desire to pursue this profession. He knew that she would not be against it; nevertheless, there was a rift, a first step toward a different world.

A year earlier, his mother had nearly died when she fell in the barn. This accident had further strengthened the bond between her and her children. Her work days were long. She labored in the kitchen, in the barn, and in the garden. She did laundry and fed the cattle, and in the evenings, Jean-Pierre heard her pray the rosary. She courageously took on the challenges associated with the severe illness of her husband. In those days, it was part of rural culture that in large families, one son would become a priest; thus she comforted her weeping child by saying, "Nothing distresses the good Lord more than lack of faith."

The College of Sierck-les-Bains was run by devout Marist Brothers who fostered a special admiration for the Virgin Mary. This was quite a different life for the carefree spirit of the altar boy who was now subject to stricter discipline, in which everything became more difficult and led him to silently suffer. At first, he still stayed with his aunt in the little town, and then he moved to the boarding school, where he attracted the attention of the principal for being "unruly and nervous." Then, however, he remembered the hard work of his parents in their attempt to come up with the funds necessary for his studies. He began to change the way in which he lived his life—at first hesitantly, then radically, so that his siblings soon no longer recognized him when he came home for the holidays, noticing his quiet behavior during meals and walks. The separation from his former life had become complete, and he believed he heard a voice telling him, "What you have loved is forever lost."

In the first years, the young high school student had two female teachers who deeply impressed him. He felt they were sensitive and attentive to his needs in view of his difficult situation. In addition, he experienced a peculiar mixture of attentiveness and gentleness from them. Decades later, he would call this "motherly pedagogy." As the time of his puberty began, he felt comfort through the nurturing attention of these women. Never again in his long life did he rave as much about women. Moreover, he was almost completely safe from any dangerous closeness to them.

Jean-Pierre relates that at the age of fifteen, he heard Hitler "shout" in the radio for the first time. It sounded threatening, and there was something ominous in that voice. Soon he saw reconnaissance planes fly over the college. As a result, all villages in the borderland had to be evacuated. Luckily, the chemistry and physics teacher managed to move the Marist students and all materials into a vacant castle near Paris. However, already by 1940, the school had to be closed.

Jean-Pierre moved in with his parents, who had fled into the rural area between the Meurthe and Moselle Rivers where they lived with their children, altogether six people in one room. Hounded by Stukas, German low-flying fighter planes, Jean-Pierre finally reached the train station of Châlons-Sur-Marne after having caught the last train. What followed was an odyssey of the family. In covered wagons and wheelbarrows, they headed to the South, supposedly the unoccupied area of France, but the Germans were already there, and on their trip back the family experienced air raids and roadblocks. "When I tried to get bread, I was lying face-down in a field of wheat," he reported. "We all feared for our lives."

Finally, the terrified Schumacher family arrived in Buding, where their mill was still standing, yet everything else was plundered. While mother immediately planted leek and pumpkin seeds, Jean-Pierre refused to do school work in German and preferred to help his father. However, soon after, people born in 1924 were drafted for the German Labor Service, so he was forced to join.

Only one day after he received the official papers, he had to report in Thionville and certify in writing that he was not Jewish. When he refused to comply, the German secret police interrogated him three times and, eventually, forced him to sign the paper. Seven decades later, the monk explains that all these experiences were "good for his calling." There was great hardship, and each day the worst was to be expected, yet in this state of constantly hovering between life and death, one felt a strange kind of closeness to God. During the First World War, Teilhard de Chardin had had similar experiences there: at day a hail of bombs in the hell of Verdun; at night, hours of grace when the fires between the trenches ceased for a while.

Jean-Pierre completed the Labor Service in the camps of Krefeld and Düsseldorf. The forced laborers lived in wood huts, and there was no chance for them to escape. The "Upper Troop Leader," a level-headed Protestant, called him "The little French." At times rocks were flying through the air, and often he heard blasphemies against Christ. Firmin Creutz from Lorraine became his friend. In 1942 when Düsseldorf was attacked by firebombs, they had to hurry to help the refugees. The following order had been given: "Whoever steals anything from the houses will be court-martialed." There were strict rules for cleaning boots, digging trenches, and cleaning up rubble. Life was hard. Nevertheless, he concerned himself with his roommates and gave up his furlough in favor of a comrade. Jean-Pierre has not forgotten those times and still today knows, "It did not destroy my calling. Even in this rude environment I remained steadfast."

After six months of Labor Service, he went on to military training in Kaiserslautern, where he declined to be drilled to become an officer candidate "in the army of the enemy." Then, in the barracks of Greater Germany in Heidelberg, he was supposed to learn how to handle machine guns in order to become an armored infantryman. However, before he was deployed to the Russian frontline for a big operation at the Maginot Line, he was, much to his surprise, diagnosed by the deputy with an eye disease that declared him "unfit for fighting." Supposedly suffering from tuberculosis, he was presented to the students of the military hospital as "a special medical case." Still today he smiles when he thinks about it: "I lost my heart in Heidelberg," for he had fibbed about everything. Finally, in August of 1943, he was released from the Armed Forces.

Nevertheless, he was left with emotional wounds upon his return home from his war experiences in Germany. When he resumed working for his father, who was not drafted for military service since he provided supplies to the population and was therefore indispensable, Jean-Pierre had lost his calling to lead a religious life. He seems to pretty much avoid this topic since he does not talk much about it, but he mentions that the reasons for his decision were, on one hand, the tough fate of the forced laborers, and on the other hand, his passionate desire to learn his father's trade. Strict rules had been issued by the Germans for work in the mill, so Jean-Pierre immersed himself in his task and invented an even better method to produce flour.

However, the war in the contested borderland had not yet ended. In 1944, U.S. armed forces advancing from Normandy and the liberated Paris united in the area around Thionville. Before the Germans retreated to the right banks of the Moselle River, they set mines. Refugees continuously streamed into the area, and the Schumacher family gave shelter to the poorest of them. As a result, father and son could only work at night, but Jean-Pierre did not manage to keep his eyes open in the first half of the night. When they changed shifts, things worked out perfectly for them. As he would later say: "This prepared me for the nightly vigils in the Trappist monastery." Then the family was suspected of working for the Americans, while at same time, the Yanks treated them like "Krauts." During air raids the family fled into the cellar. Finally, in the winter of 1944, when the Battle of the Bulge began, the Germans advanced from the Saar River to Luxembourg, and Jean-Pierre found numerous people dead in the forests, one of whom he remembers particularly well. He had read aloud his breviary, the Catholic hourly prayers, before he died.

Right after the war had ended, Jean-Pierre returned to the seminary "for reflection." It was now located in Senlis in the outskirts of Paris. There, in the silence of renewal, an important change took place. He who "had given up" decided to go on nonetheless. In a quiet voice he says today, "Mother Mary helped," but he does not want to comment more on it. There are numerous events in his life to which he only alludes; he reflects about them in solitude and keeps them entirely to himself.

Jean-Pierre failed his high school diploma exams the first time he took them. Finally, in October of 1945, he tried them again and passed. Then he spent his Marist novitiate in the mountains near Lyon. There ten novices lived "like in paradise, far away from the world" in a rich and all-consuming atmosphere. His comrade Joseph Fritsch would join the La Trappe Abbey, and an English fellow brother entered into the Carthusian monastery in Grande Chartreuse. Jean-Pierre himself felt a desire to move to a more contemplative order, and as early as in 1948, he made his vows and studied in the seminary of Lyon and Ste-Foye-lès-Lyon to become a priest.

His spiritual leader P. Vivier wanted him to study philosophy at the Jesuit University Fauvières where the avant-garde theologian and later cardinal Henri de Lubac taught, a man who was looked at by the Vatican with great suspicion. Yet Jean-Pierre felt like going somewhere else. While the other novices participated in weekends for the young in the surrounding parishes, the monk from Lorraine stayed in the seminary repairing bicycles or retreated into the chapel.

The first time he set foot in a Trappist monastery was in the context of a retreat. It was the Abbey of Les Dombes where Father Ignace gave talks about the burning thornbush. Jean-Pierre was fascinated by this image in the second book of Genesis where the Lord, "I am Who I am," speaks: "Don't come closer. Take off your shoes, for you are standing on sacred soil." This experience caused him, once again, to become fully aware of his calling, yet little did he know at the moment that this calling would lead him far away and that the time approached when his childhood dream would draw near.

Then Jean-Pierre was ordained to the priesthood. The first Mass he read took place in a deserted village, the second one in the presence of his parents in the church of Ars. After such a long journey with many detours, it was a meaningful experience for him when the sexton handed the chalice and the sacred robes to him. Jean-Pierre says of this hour of his life: "This day was followed by many gifts of mercy."

July 21, 2011

7:15 AM: Godefroid, the biggest and youngest among the fellow brothers, glides his fingers over the strings of the zither. Its sound is rich and his voice deep. He has a blond beard, which he sways back and forth. The instrument matches the early morning psalms: "Wake up, harp and string music. I want to awaken the red morning sky."

9:00 AM: Last night three Spaniards arrived. They want to research new projects for orphans in the surrounding mountains and collect money for them back home. They have come from Madrid and Pamplona; one is a banker, one a physicist, another one a math teacher. Carlos, Inigo, and Juan are all in their midthirties. We speak broken Spanish, English, and French. Soon it becomes clear that one would like to have guys like these as friends.

10:30 AM: A break in the "tea salon." José-Luis wishes me great luck. When I ask him why, he says that today is a Belgian national holiday. I had forgotten about it since our small country is so far away. The struggle of communicating in combating languages feels humiliating in view of four Trappist brothers who have committed their lives to a good Christian-Islamic coexistence.

12:30 PM: In the sixth hour of the hourly prayers, a letter of Paul to the Galatians (5:16), "Be guided by the Spirit, and you will no longer yield to self-indulgence."

2:00 PM: Jean-Pierre has always adored his fellow brother Luc, the "Toubib" (physician), for his crusty and boyish demeanor. This morning he quoted from one of the letters that he had written one year before he was murdered, "Since death means encountering God, it cannot create fear. Death is in fact God."

8:45 PM: Before nightfall, the prior prays in Compline "for all our friends whom we have left behind in Tibhirine."

11:00 PM: The last chant of the muezzin. The dogs are running around the walls of the monastery. No sleep, only a southern sky filled with stars. Ernst Jünger, who keeps me company at night, writes, "Where does one like to live . . . ? First of all, in the countries where one is allowed to read and write whatever one wants; in cities where merchants are free to keep their stores open day and night, where in cemeteries the memory of ancestors is honored; in gardens with old trees and on terraces on whose walls geckos are dreaming half asleep and still alert." [1]

It would fit the place of Midelt: reading, writing, gardens with old trees, terraces. Yet who will be the first in the cemetery?

---

[1] Diary excerpt from Ernst Jünger, *Sämtliche Werke (Seventy Gone)*, vol. 20, (2nd sup. vol. Siebzig verweht III. Stuttgart: Klett-Cotta, 2000).

THE FIRST ABDUCTION

THE TASK THAT WAS ASSIGNED TO THE NEWLY ORDAINED priest Jean-Pierre Schumacher by the Marist order turned out to be mixed. The superiors sent him to a seminary in Saint-Brieuc located at the coast of Brittany. As master of novices he was responsible for the young aspirants, a job that was not particularly attractive. But he did not object to it and was determined to let God be his guide—"He is the One who designs the plans for my future." One has to always remember this fatalistic attitude of his, for it would guide him from then on. Every time in his later life when things became difficult or even risky, he would retreat to these words because usually such situations were powerful personal changes in his life about which he prefers to be silent.

When his superior P. Martin conducted a personal conversation with him, Jean-Pierre used to answer the question of how he was doing succinctly by saying: "Everything is how it used to be. I feel attracted to a contemplative life and have been awaiting an answer for eight years."

The Father comprehended the seriousness of his calling and asked him to examine himself for another year. Several months later, while staying in Paris, he accepted an invitation to a slide presentation about the topic of religious orders and congregations. On the screen appeared a picture of the Tibhirine monastery in the Atlas Mountains of Algeria that deeply moved him and in a quite special way—even more so, since his superior expressed that very minute: "If there is anyone who wants to leave us, I suggest he go there."

Jean-Pierre knew that these words were meant for him, and he understood right away that this was about a fundamental, personal commitment to God. Finally, the difficult time of his searching was over. "The Lord knew why," he explains smilingly. Today Jean-Pierre looks back to those pictures and the words of Father Martin as the basis for his presence in Tibhirine. It was a slide that had foreshadowed so much.

Jean-Pierre knew that the political situation around Algiers was tense due to the long-raging civil war between the Independence Movement FNL and the French Algerians. This fight of the Pied-Noirs, the colonists with the short black boots, against franc-tireurs around Ben Bella had long reached France, where it led to bad terrorist attacks. State President Charles de Gaulle was caught between the two fronts, while Cardinal Duval of Algeria personally favored independence.

During the Easter break of 1957, the members in charge of the Marist order could no longer postpone having a conversation with Jean-Pierre. It was a surprisingly short encounter; they had brought themselves to let him go. The only question was where—to the nearby Cistercian abbeys of Timadeux or Boquen or perhaps to the Benedictine monastery of Landévennec north on the Cape of Brittany? The superior did not hesitate much longer, took the phone, and asked to be connected with the abbot of Timadeux, and within a few minutes he settled this difficult case of a late calling. The farewell from Saint-Brieuc took place equally fast. Still today Jean-Pierre talks enthusiastically about it. "That was my honeymoon trip." But he did not leave in anger, for his relationship to his community had been a heartfelt one, and his former fellow brothers even gave him a farewell gift, an edition of the New Testament.

From the beginning, Jean-Pierre was quite impressed with his new abbot Dom Emmanuel, the former secretary of the bishop of Nancy who had experienced the war in Germany and originally joined Timadeuc as a simple lay brother. However, since Jean-Pierre had already been ordained as priest and made his monastic vows, his move was complicated with regard to church law. Eventually, it was decided that he should be assigned the rank of a novice, but that he would no longer belong to the novitiate, and he was allowed to wear the open white habit of an oblate. Through a simple profession he was assigned the position of assistant to the guest father.

The first time he looked through the small window of the dormitory with its wooden cells that opened to the ceiling, he saw the gentle meadows and fields of Brittany, and suddenly he realized, "This is the countryside that you will see until the end of your life." But wasn't it God who would determine which road he would walk? On August 20, 1960, Jean-Pierre made his eternal vows that would tie him forever to the Abbey of Timadeuc.

Meanwhile in Algeria, war was raging and approaching its peak. At times, Jean-Pierre remembered the lecture in Paris and the hard-pressed fellow brothers in Tibhirine high up in the mountains, sixty kilometers from Algiers, the center of the unrest.

Life in the Breton abbey was hard because the old rules of the "Strict Observance of the Cistercians" were still reinforced. In the fields, beets, potatoes, and wheat were harvested. During the wheat harvest, the heavy bales had to be loaded on wagons, and all of this had to be carried out while wearing sophisticated monastic attire with scapulars and long undergarments. One took a shower only once a week. On Thursday nights, the monks often practiced self-accusation for minor delinquencies in the chapter house and were condemned to atone for them in public. Every Friday, the day of the Lord's death, the nightly office was followed by "the Discipline." When the master of novices gave a signal with his foot, the six young brothers had to flagellate their naked upper bodies in their cells. Today Jean-Pierre explains, "There was no blood flowing."

The food was vegetarian. Twice a week fish and eggs were served; at 6 PM apples, bread, and a small piece of cheese. The meal times were spent in silence while one listened to a reading. If one wanted to have some milk or butter, they had to be requested by means of sign language. They ate while sitting in a rectangle on footstools without backrests, their backs facing the wall. Their hoods were pulled up so they could not see the person who sat next to them. During the forty days of Lent, breakfast was more modest. Without having much in their stomachs, they went back to work.

Under the clock was in large letters the admonition, "*Ultima latet*—The last hour is unknown."

Jean-Pierre perceived this form of observance as "harsh, but exciting." He enjoyed the spiritual rules and the conversations with the master of novices. When they baked good grainy bread in the bakery, it reminded him of the mill back home. Each cow had a name, and the products of the cheese dairy were in great demand. Cider, a foaming apple wine, was the only drink they were allowed to have in this region.

Even while being silent, the style of communicating with each other was not less strict. There were big differences between the brothers who wore a poor brown habit and long beards, and the "chancel members of the order," the candidates for priesthood. The brothers did all the work and regularly prayed the Lord's Prayer; the monks silently and in solitude read Masses in the side altar areas after the nightly office. Yet the simple brothers were considered to be holier since they were role models for the others in the abbey. "My best friend was a fellow brother," Jean-Pierre tells us. "We worked together in the workshop. Yet most of all he loved the lectio divina at dawn, a spiritual reading in the study hall that was limited to the Bible, monastic spirituality, and the lives of saints. One of his favorite authors at the time was Bernhard of Clairvaux (1091–1153), where he discovered the following sentence, 'Nothing is doomed to die for certain that Christ could not heal through a miracle.'"

But then Jean-Pierre began to prefer the Bible to all other readings, and he constantly looked for connections between the

Old and the New Testament, such as with regard to "virginity" or "fire." He pursued these studies in three consecutive readings that were followed by meditations and that he continued to develop further. The results of his research had a lasting impact on his conversations with people in the Moroccan monastery. Today he exclusively focuses on the New Testament. "I love to find deeper meaning in these texts," he says, "and to see how Jesus lived his life. I always find something new in them."

When the reform movement, and with it a greater openness to the world, was implemented by the Second Vatican Council, the thirty-six-year-old Trappist felt it was a liberation: "I could not have been happier and experienced great joy in participating in something completely new." One anxiously looked forward to every announcement of further reforms. With a somewhat cautious delay, monastic life changed. The silence became more moderate, the sign language disappeared, and the ritual of atoning was abolished. Instead of shared dormitories, individual cubicles were established, and strict obedience was turned into a gentle dialogue. The scriptorium became a place for meditation. After the silence of the nightly Vigils, there was a Mass early in the morning that was jointly celebrated by all priesthood monks.

The General Chapter of the Trappist abbeys from all over the world that congregated every other year in the first founded Abbey of Cîteaux also went along with the new spring of the Church, which, however, was soon followed by a proverbial winter. A wave of men leaving their monastic lives behind signaled that times were changing. While monastic rules were adjusted to the reforms of

the Council, numerous of the ninety monks left Timadeuc, caus-
ing the big abbey not only great worries, but also posing a logistic
problem. Yet the order held out against it, and regional conferences
convened. In the abbeys themselves one prepared resolutions and
submitted them to the founding institution, and the general abbot
turned from "general" to a spiritual father whose annual newsletter
created new momentum. During the regular visits that took place
in the monasteries every other year, even the most devout brother
was listened to.

Jean-Pierre found these reforms from within quite beneficial, yet
there were gaps in information. Hardly anyone in the order had
noticed that already five years earlier, there was a strange abduction
that took place at Tibhirine. After the murder of the Mufti of the
holy city of Medea, located only eight kilometers from the Trappist
monastery, there had been reprisals. At dusk a heavily armed commando had broken into the conclave, and their leader had made
the monks line up against the wall. The old and hardheaded abbot
stepped forward and said, "You can kill me; I am old and am not
afraid of dying." However, among the captured monks there was
also Mathieu, who had connections to the FNL and seemed to be
"valuable" to the trespassers. When they arrested him, Luc, the
doctor in the simple habit of a lay brother, said, to the surprise of
his friends and enemies, "I will go along."

And thus a strange abduction took place. The first night, the two
monks had to hide in the vineyards not far from the monastery,
so that they could hear the bells of the chapel day and night. Then
they were taken to Taza, where they received preferential treatment

by the rebels. When asked what they would like to eat, they answered, "Cherries." It was a grotesque situation—on one hand it was dangerous; on the other hand it was not really threatening. A few days later, when Luc, the strong and grumbling one, finally fell into a depression, the guards said, "Let him go, he is the 'Toubib.'" That's how the two managed to get away after having gained some insight into the structure of the FNL. Luc was taken to a military hospital in Algiers and eventually to France. The news spread on the radio, and one heard about it even in Tibhirine.

July 22, 2011

7:15 AM: Feast of Saint Mary Magdalene. The figure of the former sinner moves me, her closeness to Jesus—anointing oil dried up in his long hair, almost conspiratorial conversations, but most of all her status: an ex-prostitute as a first witness of the resurrection. Why was she near the grave so early in the morning? Did she confuse her beloved friend with the gardener? Then the upsetting dialogue of "Mary."—"Rabbuni." Finally, an abrupt end that could mean anything: "Don't tie me down."

9:00 AM: Work begins. I hear Godefroid hoeing in the garden. The soil is blackish red like clotted blood.

10:15 AM: While having tea, Omar gives advice on how one can remove dust and splinters from the eye. One needs to dab it off with a hot cloth or press one's thumb on the temples. We smile, but he insists that it is an age-old Berber wisdom. The eyes of the Berbers are fervently black. They give even older women a slightly erotic expression. One considers men capable of anything.

11:00 AM: Jean-Pierre does not know what tiredness is. When
            he speaks, he splutters incessantly. Then he gives
            me a mischievous look to see whether I have under-
            stood his punch line.

12:30 PM: The sixth hour. The small prayer times divide the
            long and hot days into comfortable segments and
            also provide new energy to go on tenaciously. Two
            psalms, one Bible quote; small rations so that the
            day will be successful.

3:30 PM: End of the siesta and awakening into an unpoetic
            reality. The heat is overpowering.

5:30 PM: Jean-Pierre brings documents about the surgeon
            Elisabeth Lafourcade (1903–1958), who operated
            free of charge on seminomads living in poor condi-
            tions. She wrote in her diary: "To love means to give
            Him everything He expects of us, even if it requires
            martyrdom." In the context of Charles de Foucauld
            and the seven decapitated men of Tibhirine, this
            sounds appealing.

            One recognizes her on her photograph. She was
            a beautiful woman with dark parted hair, a Berber

headscarf, serious eyes, well-defined lips; on her chest a cross. 1922, on the occasion of her final ordination in the "Église Jésus-Ouvrier" ("Jesus-worker"), she notes: "Independence is not freedom."

8:10 PM: The book about Jesus by Benedict XVI feels like an interjection of the prayer calls of the muezzin in this environment, only a little more quiet, almost a little shy, yet with the big questions in mind.

9:15 PM: Hastening clouds, the wind blows back and forth like a heavy breath. After the nightly prayer, wild geese fly over the monastery.

THE ASSOCIATION IN THE GARDEN

IT CAME AS A SHOCK TO JEAN-PIERRE WHEN BROTHERS DROPPED out of the monastery after the Council, especially since he himself had waited for years to enter the monastery and was delighted about the reform of the monastic constitutions. At times, the brothers left after painful hesitations, at times unexpectedly amid night and fog. "Nevertheless, life must go on," he says, which attests to the tenacity of Trappist monks, who react rationally to emotional matters. He regarded the whole process from a more critical and somewhat detached perspective. Some of the brothers missed the strict customs that they had embraced, while others retained a medieval image of the order. What created difficulties, however, was "opening up to the world," which would lead life in the Cistercian monasteries out of its reclusive self-absorption. Jean-Pierre, who had professed his final vows in Timadeuc in the midst of this tumultuous upheaval in 1964, was resistant to these developments.

As a monk whose life as an intellectual in the stream of shifting theological currents had never suited him, he maintains, "The order is too bourgeois, too academic." To him this includes the present situation. "That is the reason for the lack of callings, so we must be to young people the place for which their hearts yearn." Originally, he was a craftsman, who did not receive his high school diploma until the second attempt, and during his academic studies he chose to forgo studying the new philosophy of the Jesuits. He viewed this strict discipline as an almost athletic challenge. His best friend in the monastery was a layman, but Jean-Pierre had a more humble and solid view of the monastic life.

The history of the "white monks" in Algiers epitomized this ideal. After all, North Africa was the land of the early Christian domain of Tertullian, the martyr Cyprian, and the Doctor of the Church, Augustine, before it declined together with the Holy Roman Empire. Later it was the Franciscans who ventured into the vibrant intellectual Morocco, after, in the thirteenth century, a tense but in no way hostile encounter between Francis of Assisi and the Sultan had come about. A new era started in the second half of the nineteenth century with the desert hermit Charles de Foucauld who, in November of 2005, was canonized by Pope Benedict XVI in Rome. Since that time, there is a chapel in the Trappist monastery Midelt that is built in the Berber tradition and dedicated to Charles de Foucauld. For Jean-Pierre and his brothers, this is a place to reflect about their adventurous origins.

The relationship to Morocco, which had also led him into the Midelt area, brought about the first turning point in the life of the former playboy and failed officer de Foucauld. Back in 1882 he crossed the Moroccan border, although in those days this was prohibited, and via Fès and Meknes, he reached the precarious Berber region of the High Atlas. There, with modest equipment, he drew maps of these mountains, which up to then had been completely unknown. When he returned to Paris eleven months later, he received the gold medal of the French Geographical Society for his book *Reconnaissance au Maroc* (*Expedition through Morocco*). Two years later, he made a general confession and turned back to the church, proclaiming: "My God, if you exist then let me know you." After some time as a Trappist in the Syrian monastery Akbes and later as a hermit in the Garden of the Clarists in Nazareth and Jerusalem, he moved to Beni Abbes in the Algerian desert. As a friend of the king of the Tuareg, he lived two years in the hermitage of Assekrem, situated some 2,800 meters high in the Hoggar Mountains. When the First World War broke out in Tamanrasset, he ended up between the fronts of the local indigenous tribes and Arab mercenaries who stood in the service of the Frenchmen, and was supposed to be deported. When suddenly men on horses appeared in a distance, one of his guards panicked and shot Charles de Foucauld; his naked corpse was hastily buried next to his hut. Later, in 1929, he was interred in a tomb that was especially erected for him and was located in the oasis El Golea.

Jean-Pierre had always been fascinated by the life of de Foucauld. For that reason he embraced the words of this man who was later beatified with all his heart and applied them to his own existence as a Christian monk who lived amid Islam: "It is part of your calling to proclaim the Gospel from the rooftops, not through words but through the life you live."

As a monk, Charles de Foucauld had also spent some time in the old Algerian Trappist monastery of Staouëli, which in the confusion of the Islamic-French clashes had been viewed as a place of stability, but had cost the lives of 5,500 individuals. The hard life at Staouëli simultaneously caught the attention of the Frenchmen and the Algerians, and at that time, the French powers and the order had agreed upon an ambitious project that not only provided for cultivation of treacherous swamplands, but also for the planting of thousands of trees; the wine that was grown on 425 hectares of land brought the monks fame throughout the whole country. Besides that, they achieved remarkable results in the area of agriculture so that, during the famine between 1847 and 1867, they sustained large parts of the population. Nevertheless, within a year seven young monks fell victim to the harsh challenges, and dysentery was rampant in the large community. Apart from that, numerous problems arose later. The monastery had been expected to be an example for a particularly moral lifestyle, but things turned out differently, and in 1904, the abbey had to be sold.

Jean-Pierre knows the historical development of the monastic presence in Algeria in detail, and he is very good with dates; only names occasionally cause him difficulties, but then overnight he remembers them. As the last survivor of Tibhirine, this story is close to his heart because it ended with the murder of his fellow brothers in May 1996, and attempts to revive the story had failed. The monastery was situated at an elevation of 1,100 meters in the vicinity of Medea and was surrounded by forests, fields, and numerous gushing springs; after all, "Tibhirine" means "the gardens." A large statue of the Virgin Mary was erected above the grounds, hence one was able to see "Our Lady of Atlas" already from a distance; to Jean-Pierre it always symbolized special protection, especially when things escalated in the 1990s and the Trappists themselves got in the cross fire of the aggressors.

Although the founding of the monastery in 1937 was supposed to give the Algerian church a new image, and although it remained nearly unharmed during the Second World War when it served as a hospital ward, its success was rather modest. After an initial increase in members—in the beginning there were thirty monks—their number declined rapidly. In the early sixties, the monastery was directly affected by the new socialist regime and had to cede 150 hectares to the "People's Republic," leaving to the community merely twelve hectares, of which only five were arable. The farm was converted into a collective because the powers wanted to diminish the influence of the church. Cardinal Duval bravely stood up against this and fought to maintain Tibhirine as the spiritual center of an embattled Christendom in Algeria.

Even within the order itself the future of the Atlas monastery created controversy. The superior general of the Trappists considered the situation hopeless and signed the official document of its closure, a document that, however, disappeared very quickly again when Sortais died the night after he had signed it. The authorities in the order who favored the continued presence in the North African domain got the upper hand, and the superior general of the Trappists called upon the monasteries to send young monks to Algeria; one of the first four to go was Jean-Pierre Schumacher.

His abbot in Brittany had not even asked him about his opinion but, in 1964, sent him, together with nine other brothers from Timadeuc, Cîteaux, and Aiguebelle, to Tibhirine. The appointment was much to his liking because the Algerian monastery was to be expanded and lose the image of being a discreet colony; it was surrounded by Islamic neighbors, and in contrast to the European abbeys, poverty prevailed here, and one had to make do with five hectares of farmland and a garden. "I was delighted about it," relates Jean-Pierre.

The departure from Timadeuc was festive. They first traveled through Aiguebelle toward Marseille where they visited the statue of Notre Dame de la Garde (Our Lady of the Guard), standing on an elevation overlooking the sea. Then the ship set out on its journey and headed for North Africa. At the harbor they were greeted by Father Etienne, who picked them up in what people called a "duck," a little delivery vehicle made by Citroën. To Jean-Pierre the drive into the high elevation mountains was something new: it was the time of Ramadan, people wore burnooses, the traffic signs were in Arabic, and a small boy was riding a donkey while digging his heels into its sides.

After a two-hour ride he stepped into the monastery in Tibhirine for the first time, a place that had been his goal for a long time. After a short while he was appointed guest father, yet many things surprised him while some were strange to him. Nevertheless, he loved the carefree manners of the Algerian children that surrounded him. Then he experienced his first encounter with the increasingly looming violence in the area, when a widow lost her two children during an attack of the FNL. After the incident, Luc, the "Toubib" (the medical doctor of the community), took on the woman as an assistant caregiver in his ward. "When Luc, along with his six other brothers, was murdered in 1996, it almost devastated this woman. Then during the funeral Mass for the dead at the church of Notre Dame de l'Afrique in Algiers, she suddenly stood in front of me and fell into my arms sobbing." This is an incident that Jean-Pierre has never forgotten.

In the beginning, the atmosphere in Tibhirine was still ruled by traditional unworldly observance. In the chapel, one still used the heavy leather books with copper bindings for singing Gregorian chants. The work in the fields was carried out in orderly fashion, and even the superior lent a hand. However, the rapport with the community was tense since one had heard that the order originally had plans to close down the monastery. Thus the propaganda efforts of the FNL were followed by a relevant anticolonial reaction. Some hoped for the departure of the monks, because then one could take possession of their property. Among the numerous critical voices that were heard, there were also those of the alleged friends.

Nevertheless, the novices could not be discouraged by this, and even in the vicinity of the monastery one began to rethink matters. One realized that the ward was for many a place essential to their lives. Amédée, who spoke Arabic and was born in Algeria, served as a "foreign minister" at the gate. He handled the administrative matters of the neighbors and as a former teacher, tutored the children who helped harvest tomatoes in the garden. The oil presses of the monastery were in high demand, as many had their olives pressed there. Moreover, the presence of the monks in the fields offered additional protection for the cow and sheep herds of the farmers.

Finally, a cooperative with five families was established whereby the land was divided equitably between the Trappists and the family fathers. Everyone received one hectare, was his own master, and had free access to water, a tractor, seed, pesticides, and other resources that the monastery provided, and then, at the end of the year, the accounting would be done together.

Jean-Pierre was responsible for the bookkeeping and in the Medea markets bargained for the best prices; if necessary, he stepped in as mediator. In these circumstances the rapport with the locals could not have been better and later during the conflict proved essential. However, it was perhaps also life-threatening. For that reason Jean-Pierre cultivated contact with the authorities and various officers of the army. After this flourishing cooperative was established, one of the officials of the Ben-Bella-Regime said: "This is almost like communism."

The community that came together within the shadow of the Atlas Mountains was extraordinary. Most of all, however, Jean-Pierre was frequently impressed by Luc. In his brown habit he would tend day and night to people in the neighborhood. This man who used words sparingly and was sometimes a little gruff when dealing with other people was prone to depression during the time of upheaval. According to canonical law a medical doctor was not allowed in the community because it would have disturbed the strictness of the conclave, something that one of the monks had once criticized about Luc after he had come back from a stay in the hospital. Luc had taken this quite hard, but he was much needed, and even high officials from Algeria came as patients into the uplands. On top of it all he did not charge a fee, was licensed by the medical welfare service, and was allowed to write prescriptions. Jean-Pierre liked the Toubib, and as the person responsible for maintaining the liaison to the population and the administration, he knew very well how much the Muslims in the area valued the crusty guy with the big heart.

Although I never spoke a word with Luc during my previous visit to Tibhirine in 1981, he was, nevertheless, the one who impressed me the most at the time. In spite of being a medical doctor, he wore the brown robe of a brother monk, even though it had long been retired by the Trappists. During the day, he disappeared, dressed in a coat, which at one time had been white, into the ward where the patients were lined up in front of the metal door. Then at night, due to his insomnia, he helped out in the kitchen and prepared the morning coffee for us, and sometimes one could hear him breathe with great difficulties after an asthma attack. It was moving to see him pray in the twilight of the chapel in front of the cross, with his bushy eyebrows, glowing eyes, hands folded, and hood pulled up. It is beautiful to see great men kneel down.

• Our Lady of Atlas •

July 23, 2011

6:15 AM: Last night I read two passages by Ernst Jünger that
apply to Tibhirine: "In the light of death the sover-
eignty of the individual grows immensely. It is already
an anticipation of the transcendental." Pope Benedict
XVI: "In the battle against lying, truth and love have
no other defense except the affirmation of suffering."[2]

10:15 AM: Godefroid explains to me that the name of the flowers in front of my cell window is "*belle de nuit*,"
four-o'clock flower, or marvel of Peru. Apparently,
they are the counterpart to the film *Belle de Jour—
Beauty of the Day* by Luis Buñuel.

4:15 PM: I had tea with Jean-Pierre and the prior whose
brother-in-law suffered a heart attack after four
cancer operations. We talk about near-death experiences and encounters with the afterlife. Apparently,
Luc, the doctor from Tibhirine, was fascinated by

---

2   Benedict XVI, *Jesus of Nazareth, Second Part: From Entry to Jerusalem
to the Resurrection* (© Libreria Editrice Vaticana: Città del Vaticano;
Freiburg im Breisgau: Verlag Herder GmbH, 2011), 65.

this topic and wrote a book about it in which he discussed the classic symptoms of the clinically dead called back to life, which included a tunnel, a rustling sound, the appearance of an exit, the emergence of a family member or acquaintance who welcomes the individual, similar to the psycho pomp (guide of the soul) in classical antiquity; Christ waiting at the end, a radiant light encompassing only love. In the writings of the desert surgeon Elisabeth Lafourcade, I read the following: "Medicine will pass, but the soul is immortal."

5:00 PM: It appears to me that the cries of the muezzin last longer during Friday prayers, but Omar tells me that their prayer times are not limited and can last late into the night. Right next to the tea room there is an area set up much like a mosque with a sign above the open door proclaiming *"Mosha Allah*—As God wishes." I have to take off my shoes and am permitted to enter. Inside I find everything rather small and covered with a carpet made from cactus fiber. On the walls there are pictures with surahs from the Qur'an. An information flyer marks in red and white signs the rights and obligations concerning the approaching month of Ramadan, and thus no one can claim ignorance.

5:55 PM: Before Vespers it becomes quiet as Dom Pierre Miquel compares the execution of the seven monks from Tibhirine with the seven young Christians who, in AD 240 after being persecuted by the imperial police, had fled into a cave near Ephesus where they were walled in while still alive. It is said that 200 years later they were miraculously raised from the dead and afterward described their persecution and the time of anticipating their resurrection. The bodies of the young men were discovered in AD 448 in the cave of the Pion Mountain and were surprisingly well preserved. Subsequently, Bishop Stephanus circulated the legend of the "*dormitio*," the falling asleep for good, a term that became common in the Occident through Gregory of Tours. The story is known both in the Christian and the Islamic tradition. Surah XVIII relates it under title of "The Cave."

9:15 PM: Tertullian, the first theologian of North Africa, writes: "The blood of martyrdom is the seed of Christianity." That still holds true, even for the seven monks.

10:30 PM: My thoughts once again drift to Jean-Pierre's morning report that won't let go of me. In this he related that when the monks were first visited by Islamic commandos around Christmas of 1993, Christian wrote a note in which he mentions where, "in case of a brutal death," he wished to be buried: it was to be in the forecourt of the monastery near his assistants Mohamed and Ali.

11:30 PM: Today Jean-Pierre read a passage from one of the last letters written by Luc, the Toubib, who had helped thousands: "I feel like a ship that will soon enter the harbor, whether through force or in peace, that I don't know. The role that I played here was quite insignificant, I was the last beggar."

GROWING TENSIONS

SOME OF WHAT WENT ON IN THE NEIGHBORHOOD HAD worried Jean-Pierre and his brothers early on. The government of Algeria had created a program to build mosques that then also began to take effect where they lived, and the area across the entrance of the monastery was chosen as the site for the new mosque. This was a deliberate provocation. However, there was not sufficient money to build it, and after the foundation was poured, the work ended. On one hand the monastery could have been relieved about this; on the other hand, Christian suggested to his brothers that one should allow the Muslim neighbors to use as a prayer room the monastery's unused reception hall of the medical outpatient ward that one could also enter from the street. So the locals fastened speakers for their daily fivefold prayer calls of the muezzin to the trees right in front of the gate to the monastery. At sunset, the monks would then join their prayers during Vespers. However, the monastery's generosity was interpreted as an attempt to achieve a certain purpose, but all Christian cared about was the communion of all of God's children. He wanted to set an example for love. To him it was clear that the love of Christ was not negotiable, but an unlimited and unconditional truth.

Yet in spite of meeting each other halfway, there was still a certain degree of foreignness between the monastery and their Muslim neighbors. First their neighbors thought the bells of the monastery were the "voice of the devil." The timing of Christian holidays also caused misunderstandings. It was a fragile form of togetherness. Although Luc, who respected the customs and traditions of his Muslim neighbors in his ward, was given the honorary title of Tschir, here and there, hidden resentment against the foreigners was felt and decreased only slowly.

With time, however, there grew a belief in the benevolence of the monks. The inhabitants of the settlement had no doubt that, if need be, the monks would provide shelter for them in the case of assaults.

However, there were not only tensions outside the walls. Even within the community of Tibhirine itself, problems existed, but out of pious respect, they were rarely mentioned in the reports about the martyrdoms of the seven brothers. Yet Jean-Pierre places great importance on commenting on them. He himself had hoped there would be a dynamic renewal of the monastic community in the spirit of the Council, initiated by the superiors of the order. Most of the monks in Tibhirine were not "stabilized"—that is, they still belonged to their original abbey in France and were, according to canon law, so to speak, only "borrowed." They were allowed to come or return to their home abbey at will, and this created a certain insecurity, especially since everyone was entrusted with a specific task in the monastery. So whenever someone left, changes had to be made. The fact that the superior was only elected "*ad nutum*" (meaning that he was not elected by the monks, who had made their eternal vows, but was chosen and nominated by the general of the order in the motherhouse) was another difficulty. Although according to church law this condition is supposed to last only for the duration of three years, the community of Tibhirine had already waited for twelve years to get permission to elect their superior themselves. During that time, thirteen superiors were randomly nominated by the directorship of their order.

Only upon the arrival of Christian de Chergé did the situation change. When in 1976 the question was asked, "Who among the monks wants to be 'stabilized'?" three men came forward, among them Jean-Pierre. Since there were already three other "stabilized men" in the community, one had reached the required minimum of six people to finally be allowed to vote, and the uncertainty ended. However, in 1984, when there was to be an election of an abbot, new misunderstandings came about because the community preferred to have a prior rather than an abbot. This was due to the desire for simplicity and discretion, which one considered to be mandatory in this special monastic outpost. The decision was made not only out of consideration for the political environment, but also based on the attitudes of the monks who wanted to be nothing but "praying men among praying men." "For years we had lived in chaotic circumstances," says Jean-Pierre, "yet I stayed, because I was certain that the Lord wanted me to be in this Christian-Islamic environment." A priest and friend of his from Blida said to him, "It is a miracle that something like this could be maintained."

In February of 1984, a new prior was elected in Tibhirine, which in the meantime had become an autonomous monastery. But only in the third ballot a decision was reached: Christian de Chergé—who in 1969 had been active as a young chaplain in the Basilica Sacré-Coeur in Paris before he entered the Trappist Abbey of Aiguebelle—became superior of the community. He was the son of a general who had been stationed in Algeria, and as a child he had seen with his own eyes a Muslim sacrifice his life for him. His mother had taught the five-year-old, "There is only one God." As a result, the spirituality of this nation had deeply impressed him ever since. In 1971, he changed from Aiguebelle to Tibhirine because he wanted to find out what went on in the mind and soul of a Muslim. His superiors sent him to Rome to the Papal Institute for Arabic and Islamic Studies that was run by the White Fathers. There he studied the Arab language for two years. When he returned to Algeria in 1974, he seemed to be predestined to carry out the new tasks.

He was an ambitious intellectual who gave presentations and sermons comparable to academic lectures, although Tibhirine was a simple monastery with a modest library, and priority was given to work in the fields and in the garden. Jean-Pierre, who carried out the more down-to-earth tasks of the community—for example, buying bread and groceries at the market in Medea—remembers, "He knew quite a bit and gave the impression that he did not know anything." The fellow brothers asked themselves, "Why does he learn Arabic although we are a contemplative order? Does he have a monastic calling at all, or shouldn't he rather be a diocesan priest in Oran?"

Before entering the chapel, Christian always took off his sandals. During the month of Ramadan, he fasted together with the Muslims, and sometimes Christian felt opposition from his own ranks and perceived some of his fellow brothers as reactionary. Eventually, he experienced a crisis and wanted to return to France, but then decided to spend two months of Sabbath time in the hermitage of Charles de Foucauld in Assekrem, which is located in the Hoggar Mountains of Algeria at an elevation of 2,100 meters. There he wrote the *Notes about Hope*, which mirror his crisis but are, at the same time, a clear statement of his times, a manifesto of his plans. Yet they show a different kind of sensibility and speak a language that was no longer shocking to his fellow brothers. It had become clear that his closeness to Islam was not a sign of personal ambition or a theological exercise, but rather a spiritual friendship expressed through communal prayers, unselfish help, and simple love. All of his brothers were invited to embrace this spiritual attitude.

When he returned to Tibhirine, a change had taken place in Christian's life, and he asked for permission to make his Eternal Profession. He explained to his fellow brothers how he perceived his calling and asked them for forgiveness if they felt he had hurt the community through his own behavior. Jean-Pierre noticed that Christian had established direct contacts to Sufis—Islamic wise men. In effect, Jean-Pierre was in charge of welcoming guests since he was the guest father. However, from now on Christian began to welcome them in a quite different fashion. Jean-Pierre describes it as a "spiritual welcome."

Some other customs were changed as well: from now on everyone ate in silence, and new rules that were informed by the relations to Islam were issued for the guest wing. Many new guests arrived, especially priests and monks. Spiritual retreats for tourists passing through were no longer offered.

The monastery increasingly developed into a place where people could encounter each other and also—insofar as one could put this into reality in a Trappist monastery—became a kind of open house. In his ward, Luc took care of the people from the entire neighborhood. Paul loaned tools to neighbors and helped them by giving them advice whenever he could, and Christian was dreaming of a community of the children of God that would develop beyond any religious dogmatism. He stood, as the abbot of Aiguebelle once formulated, "for a truly universal Christendom of the heart that excluded no one. His goal was a Christendom of friendship, trust, and good deeds." The reconciliation of people in God was to him a most pressing concern, and he did not tolerate any delay. It was something he felt had to begin there and then.

Jean-Pierre perceived all these developments as an enormous change, and he admits that the differences he and Christian had in their opinions lasted until his abduction in March of 1996. That is probably the reason why, back then, the young fellow brother was elected prior only in the third ballot; it was a warning of what was to come. "Basically, there were no major conflicts," says Jean-Pierre, "just times of tension." He interprets them as a lesson that everyone had to learn in order to accept others in their differences, just like the new constitutions of the order with the title "Unity and Pluralism" had prescribed. "The Council announced a new concept of obedience. Each person and the role of each individual were to be respected." The General Chapter of the abbots called this "a school of brotherly love." Jean-Pierre felt comfortable with it, and his personality reflects this: he is benevolent and radiates great calmness. He is a man who is not a scholar, but seeks to be in touch with the common people.

This is an attitude that Jean-Pierre shared with the older generation in Tibhirine, and he knew quite well what a challenge this was. Instead of reading the Scripture, Christian had begun to give short courses about the constitutions during the hourly prayer of Terce. The reading of the Holy Scripture took place in Arabic, and he meditated about the Qur'an. "A distance developed between us," says Jean-Pierre. After Jean-Pierre had been assigned the task of designing the new liturgy, he did not have much time to engage in erudite studies anyway. Within a short time period, he had to rewrite the text of the psalms and the hourly prayers three times. "Never again would I do this," he explains today laughingly. "French and Arabic became languages of the church, although I have a soft spot for Gregorian chants." In the beginning, the European monasteries offered no support in this respect, since they did not know themselves how things ought to be. The reform that was adopted in the end came from the Benedictine Abbey of Clervaux in Luxembourg. A fellow brother from the Abbey of Tamié helped him for three years with the wording. By then, his assignments included shopping in the market, reforming the liturgy, and taking care of the wine cellar as well as the repair shop, where he kept himself busy working on a motor compartment of a Renault R4.

Since Christian's return from Assekrem, the interaction with Muslim neighbors and acquaintances from Medea had intensified. At Christmas, boys and girls from Madagascar showed up and sang songs in several voices during midnight Mass. It moved everyone. A short time thereafter, Jean-Pierre met the Secretary General of Medea's City Council, who is a Muslim, and began a conversation with him about monastic life, such as the role of suffering "as an experience of purification of the heart," or of poverty as "a spiritual value," or the pressing of olives as a process that transforms oil into something sacred. He was director of a brotherhood of Sufis and requested permission to visit the monastery. Jean-Pierre learned that the Muslims did not consider the Sufis to be true "Mussulmen," "because they supposedly pray too much." They were also not well respected by the state, which accused them of having incited revolutions repeatedly throughout history. As a religious group, however, the Sufis were well aware that they enjoyed the support of the common people, a fact that those in power usually dislike.

Nevertheless, Sufis came to visit. They showed up in the monastery without being accompanied by women and were curious to see the community. Christian had set up the chapel in a way that it resembled a mosque. They sat in two rows that faced each other, and everyone wore his habit. The guests said their prayers and afterward moved their bodies back and forth. Then they asked the monks to pray. This surprised Jean-Pierre, because usually

Christian prayers are not acknowledged in Islam. Before bidding farewell, their teacher gave them a Dhikr, a concept everyone was supposed to reflect and meditate on further, similar to the "Apophthegmata," that were customarily practiced for centuries by their forefathers in the Egyptian desert and on Mount Athos. Jean-Pierre called this "opening oneself to the influence of the Holy Spirit."

Prior Christian did not want to leave it at such occasional and rather coincidental gatherings. Already while studying in Rome, he had conducted Ribât-Conversations with his Muslim friends. *Ribât es salâm* is Arabic for "bond of peace." Therefore, starting in 1979, Christian invited the Sufis twice a year to gatherings in the monastery, and it was decided that they would always meet on a Friday, which in Islam is the day of prayer. For that purpose Friday Mass was moved to Thursday. Some guests even came from Algiers. For several hours they stayed together in the reception room of the guesthouse with a table in the middle and benches around it. Soon it was clear that there were to be no discussions about theology because they could become divisive; rather they should focus on the paths that lead to God. Later they came up with a much more beautiful solution that Jean-Pierre considered to be especially in line with monastic values, namely "to pray together, but in silence." In the beginning, as a sign of the presence of God, Christian lit a candle. The shared silence lasted for half an hour, and Jean-Pierre remembers this moving experience: "It was quite powerful, and we were far away from the official religion of Islam."

The participants of the original Ribât-Conversations that had preceded these gatherings in earlier years also attended the new meetings in the monastery. Their cantor once again enlivened the prayer: "*Allahu akbar*—God is God Almighty," and "*Allah ennour*—God is Light." These are two of the ninety-nine names of God in Islam; the hundredth is unknown. Every prayer ended with a Dhikr, a word that should accompany each participant for the half year and that was selected together. Mohamed, the leader of the guests, said, "If we continue in this way, who knows where this will lead us." Jean-Pierre considered these gatherings as quite helpful: "All of us accepted the guidance of the Holy Spirit that turns all of us into children of God and somewhat relates even those to Christ who are not Christians themselves. We were closer to some Muslims than we were to some Christians. We became brothers."

Jean-Pierre loves symbolic images—for example, the one of the two-sided ladder that ends in heaven: "If one climbs it from both sides, one approaches each other and meets one another at the top. This expresses the justification of our presence in Midelt. The encounter on the ladder has not yet taken place, but we wish it for ourselves." In Tibhirine there were mutual invitations for meals with the imams. They also gathered at the occasion of a Sadaka, a meal consumed after a funeral. Women embraced the guests from the monastery, and men forged friendships with them. An imam interrupted his address and, in honor of the Christian guests, read a Surah from the Qur'an about Mary.

• Our Lady of Atlas •

July 24, 2011

7:15 AM: Occasionally, one knows already early in the morning that a day will be successful. During Mass a feeling of encouragement came about at the thought that right at that time the Eucharist was celebrated all over the world.

Before breakfast, Jean-Pierre brought me a book about Albert Peyriguère, the successor of Charles de Foucauld. The locals in the area pay respect to him as a *Marabout* (saint), and his coffin stands in a corner of the chapel. When for the purpose of adoration, one moved him to a different grave, his corpse was completely intact, and he resembled a Berber in appearance.

8:30 AM: Jean-Pierre reads from Christian's notes of January 30, 1990: "I only have this short day to give to the One Who calls me every day; however, how could I say yes to Him forever, if I did not give this day to Him. . . . God has a thousand years to make just one day; I have only one day to create eternity, and that day is today."

10:15 AM: Tea break. The monks are completely content among their Muslim brothers. They are all among themselves, working men among workers.

10:40 AM: Jean-Pierre sits underneath a blue sky and rushing pine trees: "Isn't this marvelous?" The doves that fly from branch to branch remind him of the Song of Songs in the Old Testament: "Oh, you are beautiful, my darling! Oh, you are beautiful. Your eyes behind your veil are like doves."

12:30 PM: Fried eggplants and chips. We eat in a different room than the monks, but we eat the same vegetarian food and drink cold water. In this heat hunger has its limits. We take turns in saying grace. Today I say it in German, like at home. No one feels irritated; then follows its translation.

1:15 PM: I love to let myself fall on my bed in my cell during the day and to feel the hard mattress and the pillow in the back of my neck, and I love to look at the flowers and the blue sky outside. I am all alone and have all the time in the world. I will not allow any distracting thoughts to interfere, other than the happiness to be here.

5:00 PM: In a letter to the small community of Midelt the French President Sarkozy a while ago wrote: "Through the Mediterranean, Europe and Africa will build a common destiny and participate in the fate of the world and the process of globalization." This is the grandiose and noncommittal language of politicians.

The prior answered with a more concrete statement: "Certainly it is our obligation to show to the whole world that we can live together no matter to which culture or religion we belong. . . . Outside of our religious beliefs there is a one and only God Who attracts us to Him and invites us to unremittingly build the world with Him, a world in which 'man is no longer a wolf to his fellow man,' but rather a world in which we recognize each other as brothers and as children of one Father."

5:40 PM: Jean-Pierre loves to tell stories about his friend Luc. For example, now and then, the doctor would have a little glass of wine, which he called a "disinfectant," and in his hour of death he wished for a bottle of champagne.

7:00 PM: Under the trees, I no longer exactly recall which psalms we had just sung during Vespers, but it appeared as if I was sitting by a brook with fresh water. On the sandy soil between the ants lies a white feather of a dove. I will take it home with me.

9:15 PM: After the nightly prayer I begin to understand what Jean-Pierre meant by the expression "spirit of Midelt": it is the spirit of Charles de Foucauld, that of his successor Albert Peyriguère, of Elisabeth Lafourcade, the surgeon of the poor, and also the spirit of the seven "Sleepers" of Tibhirine. They resemble each other because they share the same charisma: "Serving the brothers and sisters of Islam while being at the mercy of God's discretion." It is also the spirit of Christian. I still have his letter of September 1982. In his delicate handwriting he explains that his calling to enter the Atlas monastery demanded more from him than if he had entered a European abbey: it meant more solitude, greater poverty, and, most of all, unselfish love for Islamic Algeria.

Similarly, Christophe wrote in his diary: "We are aware of our maternal responsibility towards those we love."

10:30 PM: A North African night, the best hour of the day. In a distance music from a festival, wedding dances, and cries of jubilations.

"MISTER CHRISTIAN"

THE DAILY GREETING EXPRESSION OF THE MUSLIMS ("*Bismillah*—in the Name of God") gained an ambiguous meaning in Algeria in 1988, when severe social unrest was followed by security forces shooting into crowds of protesters. Even the town of Medea was aflame. The town hall and several banks were raided; students and young people were particularly involved. When in the following year, the government agreed to a democratic constitution, the radical Islamic fundamentalists of the Islamic Salvation Front (FIS) gained 188 out of 430 seats in the first free elections. Afterward the Secretary of Defense assumed power, annulled the second ballot, dissolved the parliament, and declared a state of emergency while calling the FIS illegal. Thus the FIS went underground and began a civil war against the rulers. It was a deep cut with wounds that are yet to heal. Jean-Pierre and his brothers in Tibhirine had no illusions about it: "The situation became quite precarious, and we were afraid because everyone shot at everyone, and they could strike anywhere." The Valley of Tamesguida and the surrounding mountains were areas to which the rebels retreated, and the monks called them the "brothers from the mountains." Yet the military referred to them as the "brothers from the plains." Even in the midst of the militant controversies, the Trappist monastery continued to use a language of reconciliation underneath the big statue of Mother Mary, advocating no bloodshed, no weapons, and no partisanship.

In the meantime, there was increased tension in the Islamic camp, of which the most radical wing, the GIA (Groupe Islamique Armé—Armed Islamic Group), claimed responsibility for the bloodiest terrorist attacks. The ultimatum to step down that had been given to the state leadership ran out on November 30, 1993, without a reply. Thereupon the government called upon all foreigners to leave the country since their safety could no longer be guaranteed.

In Tamesguida, about three or four kilometers from the monastery, Croatian construction workers were busy; they liked to attend the midnight Mass in the monastery. It was always a most emotional ritual. First one sang Vigils, and the Christ child was carried to the nativity set in the dark chapel. Then the prior lit a candle. The statue of the Christ child had been made from terra cotta by the female founder of the Little Sisters of Charles de Foucauld, Mother Madeline, and had a special meaning to the community. After Mass the guests were invited for tea, hot cocoa, and sweets. Everyone sang Christmas songs in their respective mother tongues, and the Croatians reminisced on their homeland because they were homesick.

But in 1993, something quite different happened, something terrible: in the night of December 12 during an attack by a GIA commando of fifty people, the Croatians' throats were cut. One survived because at the last minute one recognized that he was a

Muslim; another one who was severely injured could be saved at the edge of the valley. The shock was deep, the fear spread, and everyone asked themselves: "Will we be the next victims?" All the more they admired the courage of the priest of Medea, Gilles Nicolas, for saying the following words during a funeral service for the Croatians: "This year, the Remembrance Day for the Innocent Children does not take place after but before Christmas. Even if we remain silent, the rocks will still cry out."

Then Christmas Eve arrived. Jean-Pierre was in the sacristy getting the liturgical instruments and the vestures ready for midnight Mass, while the prior was in his office; Michel was in the kitchen preparing hot cocoa. Célestin was sorting the papers with the songs; Paul and Nicolas, together with two students from Madagascar who still made it to the monastery before curfew, were in the guesthouse. Suddenly Jean-Pierre heard strange whispering sounds. He assumed it was Célestin, whose health was delicate after a bypass surgery, but then he saw that Célestin was threatened by a young man in military uniform who was squatting on the ground armed with a Kalashnikov rifle. Christophe and Philippe fled into the cellar. The armed man had the order to round up the brothers in the guesthouse. Luc, the medical doctor, slept exceptionally well that night and did not notice a thing. When Jean-Pierre saw how they led Michel away, who was a particularly sensitive man, the following words from the Bible came to mind: "Like a sheep you led me to the slaughter."

In the front yard of the guesthouse there he was, armed to his teeth, Syad-Attia, the dreaded boss of the gang. Jean-Pierre heard a member of the flying squad talking in Arabic to the priest and the two students: "We won't harm you. We are fighting against the government." Yet Sayad demanded in a sharp voice: "I want to see the pope of this corner here." Paul hurried to call Christian, who was in his cell, but the latter answered in unbelievable calmness: "I am not in a hurry." When he went down the staircase, he said in a voice so everyone could hear him: "One does not come to this place in arms. If you want to have a dialogue, then the weapons have to go. This is a house of peace, or we will discuss it outside the gate." Basically, his words were quite audacious, but Sayad followed him to an area beyond the chapel and related his conditions.

First he demanded that Luc should accompany him into the mountains in order to tend to a wounded man. The prior refused because this could have been interpreted as partisanship for the GIA. Then the terrorist leader asked for medication, but Christian pointed out that Luc suffered from asthma and could not leave the ward. He added that no matter who came to ask him for help would be treated, and that the medication supply was only enough for the population of the village. Finally, Sayad demanded money. Christian emphasized that the monastery was not wealthy and lived off the toil of their hands. "But I know that you are rich," Sayad interrupted him. Yet he received the following answer: "We live off what we have and still give to the poor."

Then the prior dared to ask a counter question that could have cost him his life: "Are you aware on what day you appear before us? We are getting ready for tonight's celebration of the arrival of our Prince of Peace, Sidna-Aissa."

"We did not know this," Sayad answered, "but we will return." That was an ultimatum. Sayad extended his hand to the prior, who hesitated to shake it because it was smudged with the blood of the Croatians, but then returned the gesture. The two even agreed on a password in case there were other people staying at the monastery at the time they were going to come back. The secret word between the terrorists and the monk was, "Monsieur Christian."

Afterward the prior, together with the priest of the village, returned to his room. For the time being, the danger had been overcome.

Still today Jean-Pierre vividly remembers what happened back then: "We knew that, if they held on to their demands, we had to expect the worst. Under no condition did we want to become their accomplices. It was out of the question for us as monks, and we would have never participated in fights of that sort."

From that day on, Tibhirine lay in danger every night, and all monks agreed that if Sayad continued to demand money, they would give him some and then prepare their departure and leave the monastery.

Jean-Pierre was deeply impressed by the courage his prior had shown by starting a discussion with a terrorist in such a precarious situation. Christian had looked in Sayad's eyes both with determination and gentleness. He believed in the power that such an encounter at eye level could have. Soon after, he wrote his testament in which he described it as "VISUALIZING." And these words were not mere theory. Christian also embodied strength and humility. The other brothers expressed solidarity with him, and they laughed when Amédée told them that when he woke up Luc, the Toubib, and told him that the GIA had shown up, that the latter just shrugged his shoulders.

Christian searched for a solution to the conflict and, shortly after the first assault, wrote a letter to Sayad in which he attempted to convey to him the meaning and the purpose for the presence of the monks in the land of Islam. It was the reaction of an intellectual who believed in the persuasive power of the written word. Christian hoped that the GIA would give in when they saw his logical reasoning that culminated in the statement that the monks rejected any sort of militant confrontation. His last sentence read: "We hope not to die by your hands." However, the letter was never sent.

Jean-Pierre called the content of the letter groundbreaking: "Each and every one of us made a free decision to live here. We are committed to our calling until death. I don't believe that it is the will of God that this death comes through your hands. Should the Muslims, one of these days, come to the conviction that we are a burden to them, we would feel great sadness but respect their wish and leave the country. Yet I know that even then we would continue to love them and you as well."

Shortly later, Sayad was severely injured in a fight between two groups at war with each other. For nine days, he struggled with death in the vicinity of the monastery and, finally, died. In order to deter others from further violence, his corpse was strapped to a car and dragged through the town of Medea. Jean-Pierre and his fellow brothers were shocked, and Christian commented on the death of his opponent with the following words: "They killed him twice." The scenes in the movie *Of Gods and Men* that show the identification of Sayad's body and the signing of the cross through the prior are dramatizations and did not take place in reality.

In the meantime, violence in Algeria had reached its peak. Jean-Pierre repeatedly witnessed cruelties whenever he ran errands in Medea. One time he discovered on an armored vehicle the corpse of an officer well-known to him. Another resident was shot in the back by the rebels as a warning to others, although he had just been sitting on a garden bench. At first, Jean-Pierre insisted on continuing to wear his monastic habit with the hood that resembled a Djellaba, but then one day some young people in Algiers called him a French "intruder" because of the way he was dressed. As a response to this accusation, he henceforth wore civilian clothes.

The journey to Algiers that the prior undertook on December 30 was to have lasting consequences. He intended to pick up Amédée, who had undergone medical treatment in Paris, from the airport. However, due to cold weather, the runway in France was icy and the flight delayed to the following day. Christian spent the night in the rectory of St. Augustine, but he could not fall asleep, constantly wondering what might happen the next day. This question tormented him, especially since they had to pass through the treacherous Chiffa Gorges. "I don't want to die like this," he told himself. "I owe it to my parents, my community, my friends, and the church to account why I die in this way." Therefore before dawn, he sat down to write a second draft of his testament, put it in a double envelope, and mailed it to his fellow brother Gérard in Paris with the request that the second enclosed letter be opened only after his death.

There is a river roaring through the Chiffa Gorge. Amédée prayed the rosary, as he usually did in precarious moments, while Christian was driving the R4 anticipating the worst. Steep cliffs were towering right in front of them and would have offered any raiding force the opportunity for an ambush. Jean-Pierre mentions that he could understand quite well the extreme tension the two brothers felt, since he himself was quite familiar with that road, and several times had seen busses and office vehicles in flames. Every day by four o'clock in the afternoon, the military blockaded traffic between Medea and Algiers. However, on that winter day nothing happened, and the two monks returned to their monastery unharmed.

A few days later, the Wali, the prefect of the region of Medea, invited the prior and Jean-Pierre to an urgent meeting in his office where he strongly suggested they should leave the monastery. When they refused, he offered them refuge in an abandoned hotel in town. "We just wanted to stay close to the people," Jean-Pierre explains. "They would not have understood had we left them in the hour of danger."

July 25, 2011

7:30 AM: After the nightly office, Jean-Pierre had slid a note underneath my door that said, "There is nothing left to fear than the harshness of a heart of stone. Therefore the monks pray to God for 'the gift of tears,' so that their hearts might find comfort."

The gift of tears—judging from Jean-Pierre's face, he has cried many tears in his life and still does, now mostly out of gratitude.

8:00 AM: There is a great silence in the house. Sunday Mass will not begin until 11:00 AM. The black mountains are engulfed by mist underneath a pure blue sky. In the garden the flowers have bright colors, and the cypress trees are a mixture of black and green. The latter are the favorite trees in monasteries since they point to the sky.

I am late for breakfast and miss out on the coffee, so I have to do with some dry bread and an apple.

9:15 AM: While rummaging in the library I discover a book about Hadewijch of Antwerp, a Flemish mystic of the Middle Ages about whose life hardly anything is known. One section referring to life reads: "God desires to be my thirst. By retreating He lets me discover Him. By concealing Himself, he reveals His secrets, and by withholding Himself from us, He delivers Himself."

11:00 AM: Celebration of the Eucharist, headed by Jean-Pierre. His sermon is about the parable of the treasure hidden in the field, the concealment and glory of God. Whoever discovers the treasure will sell everything he has in order to acquire it. He, too, had left everything behind at the mill in Buding in order to seek a treasure. Now, slightly bent forward by age, he holds the treasure in his hands at the altar. "It will not take much longer," he says with a smile a little later, "and I may keep it forever."

The Franciscan nuns from next door brought along some women friends, and after Mass, embraces were exchanged. The three Spaniards wore their Sunday outfits, and there was cheerfulness typical for Sunday in a southern country. Inside, Jean-Pierre cleans up the altar, then he stands right underneath the icon with the "Seven Sleepers" and has his picture taken—Jean-Pierre, the only survivor who is wide awake.

In Midelt there is a market on Sundays to which the farmers from the mountains come to sell their vegetables, fruits, and eggs. The neighbors of the monastery respect this Christian holiday. Omar and his colleagues are nowhere to be seen, and the tea room remains empty today. Only the voice of the muezzin carries over to us and seems to be muffled by the wind.

12:30 PM: Sunday lunch at the Atlas. Carlos offers slices of melon and says they are the "Apéro." Tomatoes and olives are served followed by pizza of which everyone gets a quarter. The water tastes wonderful, as if it came from a fresh spring. Then there is a break until Vespers.

3:00 PM: Sunday is an Easter-like holiday here. In this remote area it is spent more peacefully and quietly than in other places. No work is done, except what Bara does in the kitchen. These are hours for reading. Jean-Pierre sits in the shade of an apple tree. After two hours he is still sitting there. When I ask him later what kept his attention so long, he says, "The Bible."

4:30 PM: I read about a young Muslim who converted to Christianity. Upon being asked what he feels when he hears the call of the muezzin, he says: "I feel neither rejection nor indifference, for I become one with Christ Who will make this prayer a sacrifice for God."

7:00 PM: After Vespers follows the adoration that is customary on holidays. The French word *adoration* sounds gentler than the German word. I would rather revere than adore someone. Half an hour in the hot chapel feels like a long time. The four monks are kneeling on the floor in front of the ostensory with the Blessed Sacrament that is displayed on the altar. Here the mystery begins.

10:30 PM: Stars above Midelt flicker slightly in a dark blue sky like small fires of eternity. The prophet Baruch writes that this light "obeys" the voice of the Creator: "He called the stars and they responded, 'here we are.'"

A cool night breeze and to the south the silhouette of the mountains. I, too, obey, speechless in view of the magnificence.

CHAPTER

·8·

INTO THE NIGHT

A
N OMINOUS LIGHT LAY OVER TIBHIRINE ON CHRISTMAS
Eve of 1993. The murder of the Croatian guest workers in Tamesguida and the "visit" of the terrorists
around Sayad-Attia the night before had left a deep impression
on the monks. Yet the shock about these events was somewhat
transformed by the holiday of the arrival of the Prince of Peace.
It was a mixture of fear and determination that led the monks
together in this small chapter hall, a room on the first floor of
the monastery that was sparsely furnished with just a table in the
middle surrounded by nine chairs. Along the white walls there
were some bookshelves and audio cassettes for learning Arabic.
Here the discussions of the small group took place, which, since
the onset of the terror directed against foreigners, were quite
harsh; all theories had to give way to the brutal reality. Previous
controversies about occasionally ill-tempered brothers or minor
breaches of rules had long been pushed aside by the real threat,
since this was a matter of life and death.

News had been received from Algiers that the detainees in the
prisons were badly mistreated. Cruel methods—such as using
water-boarding and electric shocks, like the French used to practice—had been replaced by increasingly more modern and terrible

practices. In order to get information from prisoners, they were beaten with barbed wire, whipped, and castrated. Furthermore, they were not allowed to sleep, and they were forced to drink water from toilet bowls. Those who three decades earlier had been tortured by the Pieds Noirs now acted as torturers themselves. The news about all of this spread everywhere, and the country trembled with pain.

In spite of the fear that pervaded the high Atlas monastery, from then on the situation was clear. Any hope that the monks would be spared attacks, since they were defenseless and willing to help, was gone. Even Luc's ward, a facility so often used, did not prevent the "visitors" from holding them at gunpoint. On the contrary, they wanted Toubib's complete attention. Everyone in the neighborhood and in Medea was in deep shock and felt threatened in such a way that no one among the civilian population dared to raise their voice against the outrageous injustice that surrounded them.

"We put ourselves faithfully and obediently in God's hands." These were the words Christian had expressed, to which he added, "into the night." This word, *night*, which can be regarded as an allusion to the reports about the Passion of Christ or the mysticism of the night in the Gospel of Saint John of the Cross, had begun with the events of the first Holy Night. The Trappists of Tibhirine, who every night during vigils stood guard, were well aware of the dramatic reality of the provocation, and recollecting their fundamental role as "praying men among praying men," they moved closer together. Since Christmas Eve of 1993, their decisions were unanimous. Every six months they asked themselves the same existential question and took a vote, while the blood-filled terrorism in the country assumed an unimaginable dimension. Yet their answer always remained the same: "Against all doubts, we will stay."

In the movie *Of Gods and Men*, this struggle becomes the major theme. However, there are no documents that reveal any information as to how exactly votes were taken in the community. Jean-Pierre does not comment on this topic, because it does not seem to be of great significance to him who said or decided what or when. It was their common attitude that had crystallized out of numerous conversations: "We cannot possibly leave our neighbors and families alone in this danger while we seek our safety somewhere else." Jean-Pierre does not want to give more details, but he also does not hide that, from the beginning, he had been in favor of staying.

Everyone in the monastery was well aware that their vows of stability had assumed a new meaning. It was not only a commitment to their order and their monastery, it also simply meant: "You will remain here with us." Since the crisis in Algeria, Jean-Pierre had increasingly come to the following realization: "These vows created an unbreakable bond between us and the lot of our neighbors. No one wanted to shirk this responsibility. It was part of our calling to be present among the Algerian people in the name of Christ."

His position was clear: "If we leave this place under these circumstances, we will never return again." One of the villagers had told him through a parable: "You are the branch for us upon which we sit. Where shall we go if you leave?"

During their consultations one of the brothers brought to mind the tenth chapter of the Gospel of John: Does a good shepherd leave his flock when he feels a wolf is approaching?

After the conversations with the prefect in Medea during which the monks had declined his urgent plea to leave the monastery and to put themselves under his protection, some concessions were made: from 5:30 PM until 7:30 AM the gates to the monastery were to remain locked, and a phone line to the house of the guard was set up. After consultation with the bishop of Tessier, the number of monks that would remain in the monastery was to be temporarily reduced. Since Paul's mother had fallen ill, he was sent to Savoy for a few weeks. Célestin was supposed to undergo heart surgery in a French hospital. In case they had to leave their monastery Our Lady of Atlas one day, the monks decided they would not return to France, but rather retreat to the community of Fès. Furthermore, it was agreed to send their only novice, Philippe Ranc, to Strasbourg for studying and, for the time being, to not accept further novices.

A few days after Christmas, the bishop of Tessier visited the monastery. He had hurried there from Algiers after the holiday festivities had ended. Wearing a suit and a tie he asked the monks who had gathered in the chapter hall two questions: "Do you want to flee to Algiers or Fès and simply abandon the people here? What will you tell them in that case?" However, in view of the dangerous situation, he made the following concession in case of emergency: "If there is no way around it, you should leave Tibhirine one at a time." The monks intended that in such a situation, some of the brothers would remain in the monastery as guards.

On the evening following Tessier's visit, Christian asked his fellow brothers individually to his cell to talk with him in one-on-one conversations. Jean-Pierre does not comment on what was discussed during these meetings, but that evening it became clear that the monks unanimously agreed not to leave the monastery. On the next morning, a new meeting of the chapter of the order took place, and Michel took the candle in front of the wooden statue of Mary, lit it, and put it in the middle of the table. It was a solemn gesture. Never before had there been more at stake in the Atlas monastery than now. It was a matter of life and death, but it was also a time of great mercy. There were no doubts and no fear left. All of them were determined to stay.

Cardinal Étienne Duval, who, during the Algerian War, had sided with the rebels, called and said: "The entire church of Algeria is on your side." When Christian asked him how the community should react if there was another "visit," the old Cardinal gave him the following advice: "Stand up against these people, and show determination."

Furthermore, in the summer of 1994, the monks in a consensus thankfully rejected an offer that had been inspired by the Algerian Foreign Minister and that was made to them by the Apostolic Nuncio—namely, to take residence at his place. However, they agreed to consult together with him and the bishop about what steps could be taken next. Half a year later, another vote was taken by the chapter of the order in which the bishop of Tessier participated. While armed troops were increasingly roaming the mountainous area around the monastery, the bishop thanked the monks for their exemplary presence, their relentless prayers, their willingness to take such a great risk, and their courage and commitment to Tibhirine.

Jean-Pierre mentions that after the curfew and closure of the guesthouse, it became very quiet in the monastery and almost all connections to the outside world were cut off. At times the silence had something uncanny about it, and fear began to creep in: "We fought it by keeping ourselves busy with manual work, but at dusk after we had sung the 'Salve Regina' at the end of Compline and retreated to our cells, the tension was palpable to all of us. We knew, if they were to come again, they would most likely come protected by the darkness of the night for strategic reasons, and we always wondered: Was it going to happen this night?"

Later, the Abbot General Dom Olivera expressed admiration for Jean-Pierre's unshakable calmness. During the critical hours he would sleep in the portal room and not give up the hope that respect would be shown for the calling of the members of the order: "The gate towards the street side was not locked. One could open it by moving a sliding bar. Inside the monastery we did not take any safety measures and did not barricade windows or doors. We also declined on-site military protection. In case of a sudden attack, everyone was free to choose their own hiding places, but we all had agreed that nobody would be willing to compromise, regardless of the sides. All that counted was our mission to be present in the spirit of the Lord: to love one and all like brothers."

In the spring of 1994, the slogan "*memento mori*—remember you will die," a traditional admonishment of the contemplative

Trappists during the time before the Vatican Council, became an everyday reality in Algeria. This was particularly evident in Christian's sermons at the end of the Holy Week. The Easter Triduum had never before been as dramatic in the Atlas monastery. On Holy Thursday, the prior preached about the "martyrs of love"; on Good Friday right before the Veneration of the Cross, about the "martyrs of innocence and nonviolence"; and during Easter midnight Mass about the "martyrs of hope." In the Church of Algeria the time of bloodshed had begun.

On May 8, 1994, two other members of the order were murdered, Brother Henri Vergès and Sister Paule Helène St. Raymond. The possibility of dying a violent death became more and more real for the monks at the Atlas monastery. On the occasion of the death of his close friend Vergès, Christian gave a sermon: "His death seemed to be so natural to me, so much in harmony with his long life which had been completely committed to everyday tasks. In my eyes, he belongs to the group of those whom I would call 'the martyrs of hope,' those who are never talked about because they shed their blood by patiently carrying out their daily work."

The Augustinian nuns Caridat Maria Alvarez and Esther Alonso were shot on October 23. Christophe made this entry in his diary: "At the church gate, at the hour of the Eucharist that they literally celebrated." Two days after Christmas, the White Fathers of Tizi Ouzou, Jean Chevillard, Christian Cheissel, Alain Dieulangard, and Charles Deckers, were murdered. On November 10, 1995, the "Little Sisters of the Sacred Hearts,"

Sister Odile and Sister Chantal, were assaulted. The latter survived the attack after twenty hours of surgery. After the funeral celebrations, the papal delegate, with a smile on his face and quite persuasively, encouraged the prior of Tibhirine to persist in his commitment, which showed "the potential of becoming a martyr."

Shortly before Christmas, the corpses of two women were found in Aïn-el-Ares, not far from the monastery. Amédée and Luc, who were in closest contact with the neighbors and felt particular sympathy for the oppressed Muslim women, were shocked.

A few days later, the brothers of Tibhirine reacted to the events with a report "about the charisma" of their order "in the present situation." The response they received was shockingly simple: "Violent death—of one or all of us—would just be the result of the choice we made to live our lives by following Christ."

Christophe, the gardener and poet, had set up a manger in the chapel by using the Cashabia, the tunic of his deceased friend Henri Vergès. Made from camel hair, its hood served as a manger. It was a symbol of the blood-filled seriousness of the matter, another interpretation of the "Christ child." In his diary he wrote:

"See the lamb, it is here. Soon: the marriage will take place.
In the hollow of the Cashabia—stronger than murder—
Is He: He was born amongst us,
in order to be sacrificed
while we are alive."

Two days later, he continued his entries. Remembering the reading they had during the night office, about Mount Morija in Genesis where Isaac who was meant to die prepares the sacrifice for the Lord, he writes:

> *The lamb and the dove are coming*
> *in order to free me from the flesh that fights inside of me*
> *about my life.*

The winter is coming to an end, and the foggy days are over. In the mountains around Medea the almond trees are blooming, and a warm wind is blowing from the Sahara desert. While doing work in the garden, Christoph wonders when the time will come "to be sown." On March 19, 1996, the name's day of Saint Joseph, he enters his last words into his diary: "When will you come to me . . . I will follow with a pure heart." Jean-Pierre is busy working on the beehives, whose wax he wants to use to make a candle for Easter midnight Mass. Yet this year, it ought to be a night that was not celebrated.

July 26, 2011

3:45 AM: During Vigils, the monks pray Psalm 44: "Because of Thee we are done to death all day long, and are treated as sheep for slaughter. Wake up. Why are you asleep, Lord?"

Jean-Pierre reads from the meditations of the Cistercian Abbot Guillaume de St. Thierry: "For you we reach out, for you we long." Soon there will be dawn, of which some say it is the best hour.

7:15 AM: Mass in celebration of the Apostle Jacob. Jean-Pierre says that he belonged to the closest circle of Jesus's friends. He was present in the most dangerous situations of His transfiguration and in the Garden of Gethsemane. Later he became known through his sermons in Judea and in Galilee, so that even Herod Agrippa became aware of him and ordered to decapitate him in the year AD 43 or 44. Saint Jacob is the first martyr among the apostles.

In honor of his memory Jean-Pierre wears a crimson robe. He points out that since the Middle

Ages, many people have made pilgrimages to Santiago de Compostela; the scallop shells attached to their hats, the canes in their hands, they passed Vézelay, Saint-Jean-Pied-de-Port, Roncesvalles, Pamplona, Puente La Reina, Burgos, and Léon. Thousands have set out on the journey in the past years and reported how deeply impressed they were by this experience. It is a powerful sign in times when God has been forgotten.

8:30 AM: After breakfast, Jean-Pierre brings me the letters that Luc had written to his friends, telling me they were "documents of powerful mysticism."

He had revered Toubib in a quiet way because behind the rough exterior of his everyday demeanor there was hidden a magnanimous heart and his presence had a calming effect: "At times, a gaze sufficed." The hearty man who had slept through the first appearance of the GIA members, prepared dinner in the evenings and took care of the ill and wounded from early in the morning until late at night, succeeded in making the doubtful members in their community less frightened.

I read all day long until late at night in Luc's letters, deeply moved and touched. What a man!

On January 9, 1994, two weeks after the "visit" of the gang around Sayad-Attia, he writes: "Our situation is uncomfortable and dangerous. We live alone and in isolation in a climate of violence, but the Lord is with us. . . . What can happen to us? That we leave and see God, that we bask in His mercifulness? God is big, merciful, and forgiving."

On January 30, 1994: "The Carthusian monks of Grande Chartreuse read a Mass for us. Thank you. . . . As a young man I had intended to enter their monastery; in my old age, the nostalgia remained with me."

Three days later: "We still live, yes, we are still alive, determined to remain in this monastery, a center of faith and charity.

On February 12, 1994, on his eightieth birthday: "Now I am eighty years old. One has to look at one's life with goodwill and gentleness. Each day we come closer to the birthday of our death. . . . At my age one crosses a border of mystery where the songs end and one feels the horror of the path ahead. If I don't die a violent death, I wish that a page with the story of the Prodigal Son from the Gospel be read to me. Just like him, I will fall into the arms of the Father; His mercy and tenderness will never end."

Easter 1994: "Christ shows us the way. He is the 'alley' through which we have to pass. . . . When the hour has come, I will stand in front of God as a beggar, with empty hands, covered with wounds. We approach Him poor, failing, and dying. . . . In spite of our failures in life it is an act of mercy to be born, because at the bottom of all evil there is someone. The secret of life is 'love.'"

On July 12, 1994: "It is very hot because they set the forests outside of the monastery on fire. The violence is increasing. Yesterday three were killed in Algiers. . . . I am eighty. Fear means lack of faith. Faith transforms worries into trust. Why should we be afraid? Pray for me, I will not forget you; I will not forget you."

On September 19, 1994: "Christian brought back Célestin (he had undergone six bypasses). My friend Professor Guillemin died at the age of eighty-two years, and my pain is great. . . . Death is a physical accident, not the end, but a beginning. . . . The resurrection will not begin tomorrow, it already begins today."

On November 25, 1994: "Stronger than rainfalls and floods is violence. Two gangs fought for power with their backs facing the wall. This is not a matter of dying, but a matter of not dying at all by triumphing with victory over death every single day and by breathing in God's presence."

A few days before Christmas of 1994, the anniversary of the first attack: "The longer I live, the more I think of Christ. As time goes on, I understand better what is happening around me. Previously, I saw Him in the past, now He is here in the present."

On January 15, 1995: "In the twilight of my life, I feel no regrets, only sadness over the fact that I am 'no saint,' as Léon Bloy wrote in his novel *The Poor Woman*. When will you read this letter? Connections with France have been interrupted. . . . The residents of Medea don't come to see us anymore, although the distance is a mere eight kilometers. They are afraid, and only the poor and sick remain."

On January 29, 1995: "The day after tomorrow I will turn eight-one. For forty-nine years I have looked at the mountainous countryside that surrounds the monastery. How much longer will I still see it? When the month of Ramadan begins, violence increases."

On January 31, 1995: "Yesterday there was an assassination in Algiers that resulted in thirty deaths. There are still seven of us monks in Tibhirine. Many members of the order have left Algeria. How is man to be tamed, this, as Péguy wrote, 'monster of restlessness'? By relying on God more and more every single day."

On February 15, 1995: "The monastery is an island caught in a storm, but we hold out."

On March 31, 1995: "When you read this letter, the Lord will be crucified. To fear God means to live in His presence. This fear excludes every other fear."

On June 27, 1995: "I don't consider leaving or fleeing from here. Rather I cultivate that small little place that has been given to me. Here one finds God and everything. Love is going deep. I am exhausted, but each day is a new beginning."

On August 14, 1995: "Many of our friends disappear. . . . But death is necessary or else human life would be miserable. . . . I won't see France again, but I will go to the land of milk and honey, the Promised Land."

On September 27, 1995: "The cold weather came with rain and thunderstorms. I feel a little better, and although in poor health I continue my work. . . . Pray for me because my trust in God is without limits."

On January 26, 1996: "May the Lord in the presence of evil guide us in His peace and His joy until the last day, when He will give us a sign. 'Do not be afraid. His mercy is endless.'"

On March 15, 1996: "Again there is horror and violence in our area. God does not want this calamity, and He is among the victims."

On March 24, 1996, two days before the abduction, in his last letter: "We can only last as human beings if we become an image of love in the way in which it has represented itself to us through Christ, Who as a just man was willing to suffer the fate of the unjust."

11:30 PM: In exhaustion I lay aside the letters, deeply moved. In my mind I wish to become friends with Luc since he seems to be a saint figure.

THE ATTACK

THE CONVERSATION IN THE OFFICE OF THE WALI BECAME increasingly heated, and when the brothers mentioned that in their ward they also took care of "brothers from the mountains," the prefect indignantly responded: "What, you help those murderers?" Christian answered calmly: "We take care of the sick and injured without asking where they come from. Our support has no political reasons." Thereupon the high official no longer attempted to persuade them, but he gave strict orders that the monastery had to remain locked from 5:30 PM to 7:30 AM, and one was not allowed to receive any visitors during this curfew. The monks decidedly rejected any form of military protection that the prefect offered to them numerous times during their conversations.

One evening when a suspicious person showed up at Jean-Pierre's portal house, he told them unambiguously: "We do not want any weapons in our house. Go back to the mountains."

Neither the Wali nor the weapons of the rebels could irritate them. They just wanted to be there for their neighbors and even when the situation became dangerous, they did not take sides. Although the Atlas monastery was in a state of occupation, the monks held on to their decision to not leave Tibhirine or their neighbors and stood by their promise to stay where they were since their hearts belonged to this place.

At the same time, however, they followed the restrictions of the prefecture without ifs or buts. From then on the atmosphere in the monastery changed abruptly since it was entirely cut off from the outside world. The guesthouse remained empty and when the bells rang at the end of Compline, a feeling of uncertainty and fear spread. Until Sayad's death one was afraid he would come back. Some wanted to fortify the various entrances to the monastery; others wished to build hideouts. The community also discussed the question of how one ought to behave in case of an attack, and it was decided: we do nothing. Everyone takes care of himself.

One had already gained some previous experience of the GIA. One evening, two of their members demanded permission to use the telephone in the monastery. Later on it was determined that they had made calls to Switzerland and Norway, apparently to sponsors or an international network of terrorists. Paul knew about such practices since he had previously been a paratrooper. When he offered them cigarettes, he received the answer that the Qur'an prohibits smoking, and he replied, "The Qur'an also forbids killing."

Whatever happened outside the monastery, it was different inside the walls where there was no violence and there were no weapons. Even later when people from the military wanted to be quartered in the monastery, Christian sent them out to the medical outpatient ward.

One day on a different occasion, two GIA members showed up in a vehicle at the garden gate and demanded to see the Toubib. However, when someone noticed that they were carrying weapons in their pockets, they sounded the alarm, and military vehicles arrived so both of them fled.

In the meantime, Christian followed the news on the radio. Some events appeared to be strange, and one could not rule out the possibility that there might be a traitor in the vicinity of the monastery. It was also surprising that the group of terrorists in the mountains would allow the bells of the monastery to be rung, although their sound announced the exact times of the day. Furthermore, women from the neighborhood could continue to enter the monastery, something Muslim fundamentalists would never have allowed. In the monastery, they occasionally said to one another in irony: "We are being protected by the GIA." Jean-Pierre says: "The atmosphere was funny in a peculiar way."

In the meantime, more and more assassinations occurred in Algiers. The military tightened their control and began to set fire to the forests in the high mountains surrounding Medea. When Jean-Pierre had to go to the city to run errands that were inevitable, it was always a highly risky endeavor. Cars and busses were burning, and innocent passengers had their identification papers taken away. Close to the marketplace a police officer was shot in the head and died. The crowdedness of the place was well suited for attacks, and the baker used to warn the monk: "Stay away from here. It is too dangerous here." Children threw rocks, but Jean-Pierre gave them candy. Only when Luc came along nothing happened, since, as a doctor, he was greatly respected. Finally, Jean-Pierre said to the baker: "If I am afraid of these people, Algeria is not the place for me." One day a stranger approached him and gave him his hand in which there was a burning cigarette.

Every time Jean-Pierre was about to go to the city, he would visit the chapel and put his fate into the hands of God. One day the community had gathered to meditate for a few days when the Jesuit monk who presided over the sessions said, "If anyone is afraid, it would be better that he leave." But he also pointed out that it was not good to let oneself be conquered by fear.

Jean-Pierre does not feel like talking about what went on during his silent stays in the chapel and requests to not be asked further questions about it. It must have been a time of intense and decisive presence for him, similar to moments in his past when as a child he fled into the bedroom to cry, or the situation in Saint-Brieuc when his calling was at stake.

Now he drove three times a week to the city, bought bread, coffee, and essential fruits. When the baker, who was impressed by his courage, gave him a cake as a gift for Christmas, the monk thanked him, saying, "We will only leave when the people ask us to." The only person who still visited the monastery was Priest Nicolas from Medea. He always came on Fridays to celebrate the Eucharist and to eat fritters afterward. Once Luc said to the guest, "It is the duty of a cook to create pleasure," and on another occasion he said, "It is easier to find a priest than a good cook."

In spite of this atmosphere of tense calmness and quiet uncertainty, the members of the Christian-Islamic discussion group Ribât were allowed to meet every half a year in the monastery.

It was the night of March 26 to March 27, 1996.

At one o'clock in the morning, Jean-Pierre was in the portal room in front of the building that was located in the middle court, when he was awakened by voices. They came from the front gate. There were not the usual two or, at the most, three people, but more. Right away it crossed his mind: "That's them. Surely, they want to see the doctor." As a sign of trust the front entrance had been left open, but by doing this, they also had completely exposed themselves to danger. "We are monks and unarmed" was the standard explanation for this.

Jean-Pierre tells all the details about the decisive hour, and his voice is subdued as if he is still in a state of alarm: "It was late, and I knew right away that it had to be the uninvited visitors from the mountains whom we had feared so much. Nobody had rung the bell; they just intruded into the cloister area. Without being noticed I walked to the window in order to see more clearly what was going on there, but I could not distinguish the group of people who apparently were standing in a more remote area, to the right of the front gate. At exactly that moment a shadow moved toward them that came from the small open iron gate leading to the street. It was an armed man who carried a machine gun and walked toward the others at the front gate. I changed my position to the other side of the room, to a glass door leading to the hallway of the entrance to the monastery. Then I saw a man wearing a turban and carrying a machine gun walk through the door that led to the cloister area and Luc's room.

"Assuming that the kind of conversation and the way in which the man walked did not indicate any sense of aggressiveness, I deceived myself into believing that the situation was not that serious. I thought they came to ask the doctor to treat someone, like they had done once before. At first this thought prevented me from realizing how many men really had come. Later the guard told me that there were about twenty assailants. Apparently, the others had stayed outside of the monastery at that moment. Since I had not been woken by the bell, I assumed that Christian had anticipated me and opened the gate because the bedroom in which he slept at night was not far from the entrance to the monastery.

"As the guard told me later, in reality the intruders had not come in through the gate, but through a door in the cellar that was located at the back side of the building and led into the garden. In this manner they had made their way through the inside of the building all the way to Christian's and also to Luc's room. When I woke up, both of them were already outside of the front gate and talked with the group. Christian stood in the middle of the courtyard; Luc held the bag with his medical supplies in his hand, willing to accompany these people in order to treat the allegedly badly injured. The guard, who told me all the details later, was there, too.

"In the hope that everything would end well, I began to pray, although I did not feel an immediate danger at the time. Then I heard Christian ask: 'Who is the boss?' One of the men answered

him: 'The guy over there is the boss; one has to do what he says.'
At this moment, as the guard related it to me later, the order was
given to open all the doors. I heard several people come and go
into the reception hall, then nothing else.

"The small gate leading to the street had closed with a familiar
sound. Apparently, everything was calm again, and relieved that
nothing bad had happened I went outside to use the bathroom
before lying down again. The lights in the cloister area were out.
Everything seemed to be in order, and I thought Christian had
sent the men from the mountains away and laid himself down
again. However, one thing seemed to be strange: in the hallway
and in the room next door there were clothes lying on the floor,
clothes like the ones Luc usually collected to give to the poor. I
wondered whether they had asked for clothing that they then dis-
liked and had thrown away while leaving. I had not come to a
logical conclusion yet when someone knocked on my door, the
glass door that led to the hallway. It was Amédée accompanied by
a friend, the general vicar of Oran, Thierry Becker. 'Do you know
what happened?' Amédée asked. 'We are alone. All the others were
abducted.'"

Jean-Pierre remained calm in this tense situation. "They will
not kill them," he said. "Otherwise they would have done it right
away." Besides that, he thought of Luc who suffered from asthma
and of Célestin who had a heart condition. Who could possibly do
them any harm? On top of everything, soldiers from the army had
stood guard in the mountains ever since the curfew had begun.
This provided a certain amount of security for them. Jean-Pierre

assumed that his brothers were going to be used as hostages in order to give urgency to the demands of the kidnappers.

The three of them encouraged each other, but did not go back to sleep. Becker wanted to ring the bells, but out of caution it was not done. Finally, Jean-Pierre said with complete certainty: "They will come back." It was already almost five o'clock in the morning. Then they sang Lauds together with the four White Fathers who were staying in the guesthouse: "Lord, listen to my voice and mind my plea. On this day of need I call upon you for you will hear me."

As it turned out, the raiding party had severed all phone lines and destroyed all the telephone poles in the area to prevent any contact to the outside world. Furthermore, the curfew made it impossible for the monks to flee since the danger of getting in the crossfire was too great.

Usually, at five o'clock in the morning, the first to pray came to the small mosque close to the monastery. But this time there was no call by the muezzin because the armed men who had collected information before their attack in the village had forbidden them to do so.

Jean-Pierre and Thierry Becker hurried to the guard whose house was located inside the conclave on the side that faced the street. The young woman standing in the doorway was upset and in tears. She said that something terrible had happened to her husband. The terrorists had woken him up and then ordered him to get the doctor since, apparently, they had two badly injured men. The next day, he reported the following: "I told them that I was not allowed to do this since the monks had forbidden me to come at night." They then threatened him with guns and said: "Moha, you will go and get the doctor." As he climbed over the fence, he fell and saw some twenty men who ordered him to bring Luc to them, and as he was about to say something they said to him, "Shut up."

Inside the monastery, the gang members finally began to become nervous, and their boss complained, "Where you lead us, there are only doors." The prior's room was at the end of the hallway. "Who is there?" he had answered upon hearing the knock on the door. "One moment, I will get dressed and come out." But then the GIA guys ripped the door open and demanded to see the doctor. They cut the telephone cable and rummaged through the cell. Then they arrested Luc, and the boss of the gang ordered his people to open the front gate, even if they had to use a pry bar. "Are these the seven men?" he asked in all the turmoil, and the guard responded: "Yes, so it is." Little did they know there were nine, and thus Jean-Pierre and Amédée were saved.

July 27, 2011

7:15 AM: John-Pierre's intercessions always sound a bit peculiar: they include personal concerns and the spirit of the universal church, the here and now and the time when his brothers had to die. His gestures are subtle. The atmosphere in the monastery: in this world, yet not really of this world.

8:30 AM: The young gardener Godefroid put a little bag with seeds of four-o'clock flowers in front of my cell door. He is a quiet person who does not talk much, so this was his way of showing me a sign of compassion. In the fall, he will be ordained to the priesthood in Aiguebelle. Next year when the pink flowers will blossom, I will think of him.

Ernst Jünger, the great admirer of subtle fauna and flora, praises their glow that radiates beauty from the inside as a revelation and "even shines through death masks." Through reading Pascal, Goethe, and Guardini, I was moved to realize that death has lost its horror. It is different with regard to undecayed mummies. "Why do you seek the living in the kingdom of death?"

I had taken Jünger's book along as a distraction. What a mistake, because sometimes his comments sound like prophecies. At any rate, he provides insight into topics that are not conveyed in contemporary literature. Jean-Pierre does not try to sound like a prophet; he just seeks to get close to them.

9:15 AM: My bed is a place for meditating and dreaming during the breaks, and I don't think of stories that relate to the old, cold Europe.

9:30 AM: Nobody here cares whether one attends Mass, and sometimes the monks are entirely by themselves. The three Spaniards enjoy this kind of freedom, but sometimes one sees them pray the rosary all by themselves.

If in eternity heaven exists, it is as blue, morning-like, and pure as it is here. Happiness is spending eternity in this light.

12:30 PM: The little Spanish woman prepared a big dish of Paella and, as an exception, there is red wine. Even the monks sit at the table with the others, and silence is set aside. With a smile on his face, Jean-Pierre toasts me. To what? "To the peace of our hearts!"

4:45 PM: The tea break is followed by a long conversation with the prior, who with bright eyes tells us in a short version the story of his life, the life of a Trappist who had made various stops in France and Africa. When in 1996, after having lived in Cameron for nine years, he had chosen the life of a hermit and retreated to the Alps in the Provence, he learned about the drama in Tibhirine. His decision to go there was steadfast. But the Algerian military prevented the formation of a new community and soon after, the pioneers had to leave the place in which they had longed to be. They ended up at the outskirts of the old part of the town of Fès, where Jean-Pierre lived with some of his brothers in a former hotel, a house that is basically quite unsuitable for a monastic lifestyle. There they hear about Midelt, and a new story begins.

Omar takes off his sandals and disappears into a room that has been turned into a mosque, and we hear him say his afternoon prayer. Several times, he bows down to the ground, and this otherwise cheerful man suddenly has a yearning and serious voice. Ten minutes later, he leaves without saying a word, as if he was still under the influence of this important experience.

9:00 PM: The Salve Regina sung at the end of Compline is
           always a quite emotional moment for Jean-Pierre.
           The hymn is the mother of the secret to his life.
           Several times it had saved him from imminent
           death: First when he was a five-year-old child and a
           horse had set its hoof on his chest and then pulled it
           back; in 1943, when he was released from military
           service while his unit was moved to Stalingrad; in
           1996, when the abductions in Tibhirine happened;
           and also one year later, when the ceiling of his room
           in Fès collapsed and he remained unharmed. Now
           he disappears through the doorway and I think to
           myself: "There is something paternal about him, and
           one does not want to leave his side."

11:30 PM: Pope Benedict XVI writes concisely about the
           momentous event at Golgotha: "Nobody was
           imagining a Messiah that was crucified." [3]

---

3   Benedict XVI, *Jesus of Nazareth, Second Part: From Entry to Jerusalem
    to the Resurrection* (© Libreria Editrice Vaticana: Città del Vaticano;
    Freiburg im Breisgau: Verlag Herder GmbH, 2011), 270.

THE DAY AFTER

JEAN-PIERRE TELLS THE STORY OF HOW HIS FELLOW BROTHER who also survived the attack experienced this event: Amédée's cell was located across from Luc's, next to the large room where medical supplies were stored. In order to not leave his two fellow brothers alone, Christian slept on a mat in the middle of an aisle in his office. When Amédée woke up around one o'clock in the morning because he had heard noises next door, his first thought was: *The time has arrived; they are here*. Peeking through the keyhole in the door, he recognized two figures. One of them rummaged through the medications; another one tried to open the door to his cell, but quickly gave up when he could not open it right away. It was the reason why Amédée survived the attack.

When finally he ventured out to see what had happened, he noticed that Luc had disappeared. The cells had been searched, the radio was stolen, and the cables were torn out. The same had happened to Christian's cell; his telephone lines had also been cut. When he went to the cells of the other brothers in the upper floor, he encountered the same scene. Everything was empty and in shambles. In an extension to the hallway, there was another room that belonged to Thierry Becker, the General Vicar from Oran who also had heard noises, but thought that it had to do with

Célestin's heart condition. Mohammed, the guard who stood in the hallway, gave him an alarming look indicating that he should get out of harm's way. Because he did this, he was later accused of being an accomplice, and Amédée and Becker had to come to his aid to defend him in court.

Mohammed had heard that only Bruno, who actually had his residence in Fès and was about to leave, had protested by saying: "Leave me alone; I am not from here." Since the GIA guys had captured seven monks, their boss did not accept his explanation. He had been told to get seven, so the number looked right to him.

Already early in the morning after Lauds and breakfast, the first neighbors, mostly women, arrived. Ali, the gardener, was still in hiding, and Mohammed was in the reception hall of the gate-keeper sobbing, with his head on the table. He assumed that his family had been killed. Jean-Pierre, Amédée, and Thierry Becker woke up all guests as well as the members of the Ribât so that they could immediately leave to find shelter in Algiers. Since all phone connections were interrupted, Jean-Pierre and Becker drove into the village and informed the local military police about what had happened. It was between seven and eight o'clock in the morning, and the police officers had not arrived yet. After that they drove to Medea where they were received by the commander, who first of all offered them coffee. Then reports were written in French and in Arabic, and permission was given to the two men to notify the bishops Tessier and Claverie in Algiers and in Oran. The news spread rapidly, and soon reached France and the parents of the men who had been kidnapped.

Jean-Pierre was surprised at the fact that no orders were given to alert the security forces and to immediately start a manhunt. When they drove back to the monastery around eleven o'clock in the morning, they saw technicians of the telephone and telegraph companies on a hill working on repairs. Finally, policemen showed up at the monastery. Jean-Pierre, Amédée, and the gardener were interrogated, an on-site inspection was conducted, and pictures of the raided cells were taken. All day long the phone rang, and the General Vicar was busy in the kitchen, where he discovered a pot with thirty liters of red bean soup that Luc had prepared right before the abduction.

In the afternoon some essentials—like bedding and personal items—were loaded on military vehicles. In an attempt to gain respect, the soldiers pointed their machine guns at the monastery; there was still, after all, an alert. The two monks and Becker wanted to spend the night in the rectory, but they were not allowed to do so because reservations had been made for two rooms in a hotel. There they prayed Compline in the evening while a guard with a machine gun at the ready was posted in front of the door.

Jean-Pierre and Amédée intended to return to the monastery the next day and to stay there. They still hoped for a quick release since they were sure the Algerian and French governments would do everything in their power. But the military forces insisted on taking the two to Algiers. The last meal in the monastery was the leftover bean soup. All they had to do was heat it up, and they said among themselves, "Luc has cooked for us." Afterward Jean-Pierre put

together the last few important items: documents, liturgical vestments, and chalices. Then the door to the chapel was barricaded,
and they drove at high speed to Algiers. At every intersection there
were military personnel who granted them the right of way, and
they tore through the streets as if it was a matter of life or death.

First the two brothers were housed in the palace of the bishop
of Tessier, where they were treated like guests of honor. Jean-Pierre
had not had the time to fully grasp the new situation because he
constantly had to answer questions, be available to the authorities,
and make decisions. When he finally had time to reflect, he still had
not changed his opinion about the abduction. He still pictured the
seven monks in a somewhat safe place and hoped to soon receive
a sign that they were still alive so that negotiations could begin.
He did not dare to think that something very bad had happened.
For him it was a question of trust in God during this time when
they had received so much help. In addition, Amédée was right by
his side; Jean-Pierre had often called him the "foreign minister" of
the monastery, and even now he continuously reported to him the
most recent information.

Three days after the raid, the three brothers moved into the
library of the Episcopal student dormitory called the "Glycines."
It was a large square building with a garden in the middle, and it
resembled a monastery. The two read the hourly prayers together,
and in the evenings, Amédée translated the news of the Algerian
television. They were always up-to-date on events. Jean-Pierre says:
"We knew more than the French press." But still nothing happened, so they decided to wait until the end of April. If by then

nothing new was heard, they would relocate to Morocco and join their small community in Fès, to which Bruno, who mistakenly had been abducted, belonged.

The general abbot of Argentina, Bernardo Oliveira, who had always shown sympathy for Tibhirine, sent a personal advisor who was supposed to not only assist them, but to also establish contact with the government. It was the general procurator of the order, the Canadian Armand Veilleux from the Belgian Abbey of Scourmont near Chimay. He had developed a special bond with the community after he had visited it during a regular visit a few months prior, from January 12 to January 19, 1996. All over the world each Trappist monastery receives such visits every other year, during which on-site discussions with members take place and internal and external questions are clarified. It is both a fatherly and administrative visit.

On January 19, 1996, Dom Veilleux had read his final report to the community of Tibhirine, the so-called Carte de Visite, in which he emphasized first that he had come "as a brother to brothers" and that he felt it was a gift of mercy to visit with them at such an important point in time: "The roots in the Algerian soil and its people run deep." He remembered the dramatic murder of the twelve Croatians in Tamesguida, only four kilometers from the monastery, as well as "the visit from the brothers in the mountains" at Christmas of 1993. He interpreted the visit of Bishop Henri Tessier, who participated in this encounter for one day, as a sign of solidarity. The endangered community whose members, through prayer and dialogue, had come to the decision that they would stay, experienced one of the best moments in their history.

Jean-Pierre especially valued that Dom Veilleux during his visit held an "unsympathetic view of heroism. According to him, heroism does not consist in performing exceptional deeds, but in continuing to do the simple things even then when the conditions have changed and one has to count on the possibility of tragic consequences." "I don't think that any of you would wish to die a violent death," he had said during his visit, "but I do believe that every one of you would accept it as a possible result of your decision. This composure gives you true peace."

The nine brothers listened in great silence to the report of their visitor. This was not about being evaluated by an official examiner, but about a serious affirmation of the life choices they had made. Dom Veilleux proved to be a true friend during these hours. Two months before the critical attack, his text read like a eulogy about their risk-filled lives: they showed obedience to the order in a remote area while being in great danger. Already back in March of 1994, during a conversation between the General Abbot Bernardo Oliveiro and the prior of Tibhirine, the prior had answered the decisive question "to stay or to leave" with the following words: "The order needs more monks than martyrs." After a little pause, Christian said with a smile: "The two are not incompatible." At the latest after Dom Veilleux's visit, the situation was clear, and the brothers unanimously agreed to stay. The order was informed, and the inevitable took its course.

On April 30, 1996, five weeks after the abduction, the bishop of Algiers, Monsignore Tessier, called together a small group of people to decide the future of Tibhirine. Besides Jean-Pierre and Amédée, the General Vicar Thierry Becker, the hermit Robert from the neighboring monastery, the Priest Nicolas from Medea, and also the guard of the house were present. Everyone agreed that Amédée should remain in Algiers in order to check the conditions in the monastery every ten days, as he was permitted to do by the prefect. Amédée was especially suited for this task since he was a citizen of Algeria, spoke Arabic, and knew all neighbors.

Jean-Pierre was to take care of the small community in Fès, since they had been without a prior two months after Bruno had been abducted with the other six monks. He realized that he was about to assume a new role and felt somewhat hesitant about it, and when he bid farewell in Algiers, it was clear to him: "I will never see this country again."

A few days earlier, a tape recording with a message from the seven kidnapped monks had been passed on to the French Embassy from the Secret Service. Bishop Tessier recognized the voices of his brothers right away. Christian was the first to talk: "Today is April 20. It is eleven o'clock in the morning. I am Brother Christian, the son of Monique and Guy de Chergé and fifty-nine years old, a monk in the monastery of Tibhirine and prior of the community. We want to inform you that we have become hostages of the Mudschahedin, the Jamaa Islamiya. We are alive and in good health." What followed were voices of the other monks who repeated the same basic text. Only Luc had the courage to express protest: "What stuff is this that I am supposed to read?" Finally one heard Christian's voice again, who pointed out the demands of the abductors to release prisoners because "otherwise we will not return."

July 27, 2011

6:30 AM: I only slept a few hours and read a long time about the history of the North African church and about its early heroes, Tertullian, Cyprian, and Augustine, then about the migrations of the peoples, invasions, massacres, and religious wars. The church has always withdrawn, and the four monks of Midelt belong to the "small remainder" that is left. Jean-Pierre personifies humility and goodness. During the night one could hear music, people dancing, and women rejoicing. It seems like many people still want to get married right before the beginning of the month of Ramadan.

9:30 AM: Under the mulberry tree with Viola, a Swedish woman who is married to a Moroccan dentist. Both of them are Catholic. It is strange when a beautiful woman talks so passionately about Christ. Jean-Pierre is her spiritual father.

10:15 AM: Baha, the dear cook, always answers with "*Bismillah*—in the name of God." Her words always remind Jean-Pierre of Jeanne d'Arc's battle call when she went to war. He says it was her "prayer for Jesus," as it was prayed on Holy Mount Athos, and that it sanctifies a day.

11:00 AM: In order to clarify the actual course of events that took place during the night when the abductions took place, Jean-Pierre draws with his finger Moroccan motifs on the tablecloth. He assumes that I still remember my stay here thirty years ago, and he leads me back and forth through hallways and building additions, gardens and gates. On the tablecloth remains a multifold landscape of time and space.

2:15 PM: I love my small desk that prevents my lack of organization from getting out of control. The most difficult and also heaviest book is *Christian's Addresses from the Years 1986 to 1996*. His last chapter deals with the "Charisma of Martyrdom."

6:40 PM: Before Vespers I take time to reflect about Jean-Pierre and his fear that due to his belief in good he might have "missed" the abduction during the night from March 26 to March 27, 1996. He had even gone back to sleep. If one sits across from him, one can better understand this. Jean-Pierre represents a humility and a belief in goodness, both traits that can somewhat upset the rules of normal communication. Yet he is not the fool, but the others are.

Godefroid drags the heavy hose into the garden. Based on his tall and lean figure, the red head, and his strict discretion, he could easily belong to the first generation of the pioneers of Cîteaux. He follows the ascetic rule of "Work and Pray."

7:10 PM: After Vespers Jean-Pierre reads the following intercession under the pine trees: "For the Jewish nation, may it keep its covenant and see the light of Jesus Christ one day." This is a rather dangerous statement to make in an Islamic country.

9:30 PM: In the Cistercian magazine are the obituaries of the Trappist monks André Louf and Charles Dumont. Shortly before his death, Father André had exclaimed: "Christ—Christ—Christ." My fatherly friend died in the night of Christmas Eve 2010 after the midnight Mass. His letters and poems have gained a quite peculiar meaning of their own.

CHAPTER

·11·

THE BLOOD OF THE BROTHERS

THE MORNING OF MAY 21, 1996, A COMMUNIQUÉ BY THE Emir of the GIA was passed on to the press. The text began with the citation of two hadiths by the Prophet Mohamed and a verse from the Qur'an about "the one who does not keep his promise." It was an authentic document and the wording left no doubt about the brutal reality of what had happened.

On March 27, 1996, seven French monks were abducted in the region near Medea. They were taken to the mountains, far away from the apostates who did not succeed in finding them, in fact did not even make an attempt to do so.

On April 18, 1996, we sent a communiqué in order to take responsibility for the abduction. Our communiqué was addressed to the French president and meant to inform him that the monks were alive and willing to be exchanged in turn for the prisoners, among them brother Abdelhak Layada. Thus we have made clear that we would be willing to release the hostages, if the prisoners were released. Otherwise, we would cut the throats of all hostages.

On April 30, 1996, we sent a negotiator to the French embassy who turned in the following items:

• *an audio cassette that proved that the monks were still alive;*

> • *a written message in which we set up the rules for the negotiations for the possibility of getting their prisoners back alive.*
>
> *First they answered us with an affirmative message that was signed and sealed.*
>
> *At that time we thought that they were truly concerned that the seven monks would be returned safe and unharmed.*
>
> *However, a few days later, the French president and his foreign minister announced that they were unwilling to conduct any dialogue or negotiations with the GIA. Thus they broke off communication and, as a result, we decapitated the seven monks as we had threatened to do and had pledged to do to our God.*
>
> *Praise be to God.*
>
> *This was carried out in the morning of Wednesday, May 21.*

(What follows are the 29th surah of the Qur'an and a hadith by the Prophet.)

May 21, 1996
The Emir of the GIA (with the seal of the GIA)

Although the terrible news, and the way in which the massacre was justified as a religiously motivated act, were the breaking story of news stations all over the world, Jean-Pierre, who was in Fès, had no idea about it in the first hours after the announcement. Contradictory stories circulated, and finally, there was a call by the bishop of Tangier, who asked for more information. Eventually, one of the brothers who had run errands in the city returned and related the rumors.

In the former "Hotel Bellevue," situated in the old part of the town of Fès where the Trappist community monks now lived as well as they could under the given circumstances, the telephone rang all day long. But Jean-Pierre and the others had begun not only an external but also an inner emigration. The news had come as a shock to them. At the same time, they felt it was fate that had taken its course, and they asked themselves why the unthinkable and predictable really had happened. On one hand appalled by the horror about the brutal deaths and the bloodshed of their brothers; on the other hand, they already began to sense the amazing first glimmer of Easter.

Nonetheless, there was a dramatic scene when, during Vespers, the youngest monk in the community came in, fell down on his knees in front of the altar, and sobbingly said, "The brothers have been killed." Jean-Pierre responded by observing him in his own unique calmness that he so often displays: what has happened affects him, but he does not allow the consequences to get to him. For he knows that it won't destroy him, since there are deeper emotions of a quite different kind that surface if one gives it a little bit of time.

So on that evening while they were doing the dishes, he held the crying brother in his arms and said, "Don't be sad. What has happened here is something amazing, and we have to live up to the greatness of it." This was a critical situation in his life and also in the life of the Trappist monks in the monastery Our Lady of Atlas. Since the monks had died for their faith, the color of the liturgical vestments during the funeral Mass was not to be purple, but had to be red, the color of martyrdom. Interestingly, Jean-Pierre thought of Cyprian during this hour, whose hangman trembled as he lifted the ax and whose blood was collected with woven fabric right after his execution to serve as a relic, and for whom, after a candle procession, a big evening celebration was held. The day of death ends with a liturgical ceremony.

Rarely had I seen Jean-Pierre talk in such a calm and emphatic way during our long conversations: "To me, they were already martyrs. I adore this deep inner joy that comes from somewhere else."

Jean-Pierre returned to Algiers once more, traveling a thousand miles through the sweltering heat of North Africa, in order to attend the funeral ceremony, but the tragic events did not want to come to an end. Six days after the deaths of the monks on May 27, the aged Cardinal Léon-Étienne Duval who had been quite upset about the horrible events in Tibhirine, died in Algiers. His death came as a shock even to people beyond Algeria. Already in 1956, Duval had publicly favored the right of autonomy for the Algerian people and when he had argued for the release of terrorists, the French had called him derisively "Mohamed Ben Duval." In 1966, without ever having applied for it, he received Algerian citizenship. It was a sign that he was respected by the Algerian government. Furthermore, as a French cardinal outside of France, he enjoyed a great reputation during the Vatican Council and among the conclave that followed.

Duval's relationship to the monks of Tibhirine had not only been heartfelt, but was also a true friendship. He loved this Christian outpost whose members did not aspire to proselytize their Muslim neighbors, but rather served them and, at the same time, offered spiritual support to the Algerian church. Jean-Pierre had always been deeply moved by his visits to the monastery and preserved the memory of them. "He loved us," he says. The monks knew how to value that this lean and courageous man fully supported their understanding of existential questions and that he encouraged them by saying, "He, the Lord, will remain here *usque in aeternum*—forever and ever."

Yet even then the shocking events did not end. When Jean-Pierre, who by now lived in the House of the Bishop, met again the procurator of the Trappist order, Dom Armand Veilleux, the latter, in his dry Canadian way, told him the following news: "The brothers have been found, but only their heads." Before noon, Jean-Pierre, together with the ambassador, the general consul, Bishop Tessier, General Abbot Dom Bernardo Oliveira, and Brother Amédée, went to the military hospital AinNaadja in Algiers in order to take custody of the coffins of the seven brothers. However, this visit was not just a pious gesture; there was also reason for mistrust.

Allegedly, for reasons of piety and in order to spare him the horrible sight, Amédée had been persuaded to not enter the morgue. So he sat down in front of the door and prayed the hourly prayer of Terce. The authorities had placed the coffins next to each other, and they had already been closed, with a rose lying on each of them. Dom Bernado requested that the colonel open the coffins, but the latter refused, saying they had already been sealed, yet Bernado insisted on the carrying out of his request. He was told, however, that the personnel in charge of it had already left the hospital. In spite of this, the Argentinean bishop remained unswerving since he was familiar with the practices of South American drug lords to deceive the public with empty coffins. However, when talking with the colonel he just claimed that he was obliged to make sure that the monks were officially dead due to the fact that he was responsible for contacting their families. Only then the order was given to open the coffins.

The general abbot and the procurator shrank back when they saw that indeed in the coffins on the felt cloths there were only the heads of the seven monks. Christian and Luc were still recognizable. Then a doctor from the French embassy was called to identify the corpses and to issue the death certificates. According to him, the heads had already been buried ten days earlier. Dom Olivera remembers the grim situation: "We could not help but think of John the Baptist. It was shocking, but within twenty minutes, everything was over."

After the death of Cardinal Duval, it was clear that his funeral had to take place together with the funeral of the seven Trappist monks, and the Bishop Tessier declared that the church Notre Dame de l'Afrique was the right place for the funeral ceremony. The cardinal had been in love with this church that was a place of pilgrimage and had just been renovated with the help of the Algerian government. Jean-Pierre refers to these circumstances as "a quite beautiful story," rich in symbols. In a time of death, Christians and Muslims alike came together in front of a church that was dedicated to Mary.

At the funeral, countless priests in their red robes stood around the altar. Pope John Paul II had sent Cardinal Arinze to Algiers as his ambassador. Next to him stood the archbishop of Paris, Cardinal Lustiger. In addition, numerous high-ranking representatives of the State of Algeria were present. Jean-Pierre wore a robe that his neighbors from Tibhirine had made for him. He says he has rarely been as moved as in the moments when the families of the deceased stood in front of the coffins on which their photographs had been placed. They all were portraits of joy and confidence in life: seven bright faces.

Interestingly, prior to the funeral there were further disagreements between the church and the representatives of the government. The latter was in favor of burying the dead on the Christian cemetery in Algiers, but Dom Oliveira insisted that the monastery of Tibhirine was the only place to be considered as the burial site. The abbot general exerted his authority during these hours. He had been warned by the incident of the identification process, and from hour to hour, he became increasingly suspicious. The authorities strove to make sure that nothing that went on behind the scenes would reach the public.

For fear that there might be an attack on the funeral convoy, an order was given that a military plane should make the transfer of the coffins to their final destination. No more than thirteen passengers were allowed aboard the plane; among them were the bishop of Algiers, the abbot general and the procurator, the French ambassador, family members of Christophe, as well as the two survivors, Jean-Pierre and Amédée. During the whole flight,

Amédée withdrew into himself, praying the rosary. After they had landed in Ain-Oussera, the motorcade was escorted by police and protected from above by a helicopter all the way to Medea. From there they continued to the monastery, where they were welcomed by the Wali.

In spite of the festivity, Dom Oliveira had to intervene again when the hearses arrived, because the prefecture had decided that the third gate underneath the building was to be used when entering the monastery, since it led straight to the cemetery that was located in the interior court. However, the abbot general, who felt at home in this place, decided that the coffins should first be taken to the chapel. As a result, about thirty firemen who carried the coffins had to wait for a while in front of the entrance, because the door was still barricaded. Then they placed the coffins in a half circle around the altar. Jean-Pierre had asked Christophe's sister to do the reading. It was the "Story about the Good Sinner" that Luc had loved very much: "In truth I tell you, today you will be with me in paradise" (Luke 23:39–43).

Priests who were their friends and many officials had gathered in front of the open graves. Every detail of the ceremony had been planned meticulously. The coffins were lined up according to the dates when the deceased had joined the order, and then lowered into the ground with ropes according to Trappist tradition. The abbot general spoke the farewell words that were followed by some speeches in Arabic. Jean-Pierre stepped forward and thanked everyone for participating in the ceremony and for their condolences. Against the will of the military, neighbors also attended the ceremony. "We have a certain responsibility here," Jean-Pierre said emphatically. This was the reason why, at the very end, there was another emotional situation that deeply touched his heart. Men from Tibhirine filled the graves with earth while passing the shovels to each other in their respective lines, according to Muslim tradition. "This is a sign of respect," Jean-Pierre adds. When finally everyone embraced each other, Jean-Pierre noticed suddenly that even the Sufi of Medea had tear-filled eyes.

July 28, 2011

7:15 AM: Jean-Pierre says at the beginning of Mass: "Every one of us is surrounded by a crystal. Deep inside waits Christ, unreachable by sin."

8:00 AM: Today is the third anniversary of Amédée's death. In 1996, together with Jean-Pierre, he had escaped the kidnappers. Of Italian-Maltese descent, he was born in Algeria and spoke an Arabic dialect. Due to his dark complexion and his little goatee, he resembled a converted Muslim. During my stay at Tibhirine, he had told me with a smile: "Isn't this a wonderful place to lead the life of a Cistercian monk?"

Amédée had excellent connections to the outside world and a good instinct for the morale in the neighborhood. On Sunday before the abduction, he said to Christian: "I feel that things will go wrong."

Jean-Pierre and Amédée got along very well. Every time Christian would give talks that were too academic, they would communicate with each other by unnoticed winks of their eyes. In 2008, doctors in the hospital of Montélimar diagnosed him with a benign brain tumor, but he was too old to have surgery. Then he gradually lost his voice until, in the last stage, he could barely speak during the Eucharist. He stayed in the Abbey of Aiguebelle, his mother monastery, and prepared himself to die by praying the rosary. Father Jacques, who accompanied him during these difficult hours, tells me that one day after the doctor had made the rounds, he fell into a coma.

Jean-Pierre says reflectively, "He would have liked to be buried here since he had lived for so many years with the Muslims." How does one experience this kind of loss of a fellow brother? "One is sad when the seat is empty." Amédée forgot his prayer book in Midelt, so Jean-Pierre took a picture with a Mother Mary icon out of it. When Amédée departed for France in order to check into a hospital, Jean-Pierre had told him at the gate, "God is the One Who drives you, and He is a good chauffeur."

8:45 AM: Time for Terce, "the third hour." Guest Father José-Luis, who likes to talk after breakfast, instinctively gets up and hurries to the bell. His inner clock is tuned to the hourly prayer, and he is quite proud that he has never missed one.

9:15 AM: Prudi, the small woman from Andalusia, left today after the vigil. Yesterday evening all of us bid her farewell and embraced her. I told her that she was a beautiful role model for praying because she was always present at prayer times, even at the nightly office. She sings the songs in a high voice and kneels on the floor during the adoration. She is a woman with determination who would never give up her newly acquired faith.

9:45 AM: Viola, the blond woman from Casablanca, showed me the chapel on the first floor of the guesthouse. It is gorgeous and just large enough for a dozen visitors. If one opens the sliding window behind the bars, one can see in an alcove the Blessed Sacrament with a bright Holy Host set in a silver cross. All around are cushions, and on an icon there is a serious, inward-looking Christ. A guitar lies on the floor, and there are rugs everywhere so one can lie down and spend the whole night there.

2:00 PM: A siesta with open eyes. The text about the exciting life of P. André Louf that I read during the night continues to resonate with me. I need the example of strong men. That is the reason why I had also taken along the books by Pope Benedict and Ernst Jünger. They tested their limits—one of them in a gentle manner, the other one defying death. By the way, both of them feel the mocking criticism of their time breathing down their necks.

9:30 PM: I sit outside on my little wooden bench. Rarely was the star-filled sky so comforting. We are surrounded by magnificence that is unreachable and yet a promise that is quite close.

11:30 PM: As a gift Jean-Pierre gave me the book by Raymond Mengus from Strasbourg, the translator of Bonhoeffer's work, entitled *A Sign on the Mountain*, the recent history of the monastery in Midelt. The author writes about the monks: "They seem to be asking mainstream Christianity: And you, what conclusions do you draw from your convictions?"

·12·

SEVEN HEADS

ON JUNE 4, THE DAY WHEN THE SEVEN BROTHERS WERE buried in the cemetery of Tibhirine, the military was quite afraid of a potential further attack by the GIA. There were armed soldiers with walkie-talkies everywhere—on the roofs of the monastery, on the balconies, and in front of the gates—and helicopters were flying over the mountain region. These were constant overreactions, but the authorities wanted to make sure they would prevent anything from happening that might spread the devastating news about "conditions in Algeria" any further. "Algeria—The Syndrome of the Slit Throats" was the headline in the World Press.

From then on, the curfew for the visitors was strictly monitored. Questions regarding future procedures that Jean-Pierre asked the prefect remained unanswered. Although he and Amédée were allowed to bring more things to safety, everyone had to leave the monastery by four o'clock in the afternoon. The two surviving monks returned to Algiers first by car, driving over remote mountain slopes; then they hastily climbed into a military vehicle that took them back to the capital. In the days before and after the funeral, Jean-Pierre and Amédée were the best-guarded people in all of Algeria.

On June 5, 1996, when the two gathered in the diocesan house
of Algiers for a conversation with the Abbot General Oliveira in
order to discuss the future of the Atlas monastery, the decisions had
already been made. In their typically Trappist obedience, they did
not disagree with anything. "The Atlas Monastery will continue
to exist," Dom Bernado said, "but in Fès." Still, before an official
election, Jean-Pierre was nominated by the community to be the
responsible prior "*ad nutum.*" From Algiers, Amédée was to act
as the general administrator of the monastery of Tibhirine. Those
were impressive titles, and they did have an effect on the Algerian
bureaucrats. Later on, the abbot general had a personal request. He
asked Jean-Pierre to write profiles about the seven murdered brothers. Already in these restless days, he thought about what would
endure.

It was typical for these ascetic Argentineans to act suddenly after
initial deep contemplation, for the most part resolutely, sometimes
emotionally. Jean-Pierre had noticed this already when they departed
after the couscous meal that followed the funeral. Oliveira went once
more into the chapter hall and took a small cross made out of two
branches. It belonged to Jean-Pierre, who had received it from the
female novices of the convent in Carpentras. Originally, it was hung
up in his cell. In the helicopter that took them back to Algiers, the
abbot general gave the cross to Claire de Chergé, the youngest sister
of Christian, who later sent it back to Jean-Pierre. In her letter she
wrote: "I love them all with the love that I have for Christ."

Jean-Pierre perceived Dom Bernardo's request to write the
portraits of the seven brothers as a lasting document for the order

and to posterity, not only as an honor, but also as a personal challenge. It was not a matter of writing a strict chronology of the Trappist order, but rather an evaluation of the events. He was supposed to not only describe the seven "heads," but to communicate what he calls the "inner character." The writing shows Jean-Pierre in a role to which he is unaccustomed, the role of an author who is deeply moved but still sets his own feelings aside und makes an effort to give a sensitive interpretation of their different personalities. His text is likewise a skillful attempt to come close to the truth, an attempt that goes beyond all other reports regarding these events and conveys a strong sense of authenticity. He begins by stating that the circumstances of the abduction in the night of March 26, 1996, were never clarified and that those fifty-six days of imprisonment and, eventually, their deaths were surrounded by a mystery. Jean-Pierre himself is part of this mystery, because the question remains: Why did the others have to die; why not he? This reference in the short, summarizing introduction is important for later analyses about the sequence of the dramatic events.

In his text, Jean-Pierre calls the prior of the monastery, Dom Christian de Chergé, the spiritual father of a spiritual path who was able to lead the community to the point where they could see clearly, stand up for reconciliation and charity, and in this context, also accept the possibility of martyrdom.

Christian came from an aristocratic family in France and had seven siblings. His father was an officer in the military, and during the Second World War, the family had lived in Algeria for three years. Later during the Algerian War, Christian served in the military as an officer himself and, in order to do that, interrupted his studies in the seminary of the Carmelites in Paris, where he had begun studying in 1956. Already as a child he was determined to later become a priest.

During the Algerian War, Christian had a revelationary experience: back then his friend Mohammed, who was a Muslim, once saved his life when they took a walk together and Christian was attacked by rebels. Mohammed had placed himself between his friend and the gun barrels that were directed at him, assuring them that this soldier was a good man. The rebels then pulled back—but the next day Mohammed was found in the village where he had lived with his wife and ten children, his throat cut. In retrospect, Christian considered this courageous intervention that caused his friend's death as the biggest act of love that he had ever experienced in his life. Jean-Pierre reports that there was a type of "blood bond" between the young Frenchman and the Algerian. This bond had become even stronger after the death of his Muslim brother. To Christian, Tibhirine was a place where he could "live out" that bond and combine his personal concern with the calling of the community.

The experiences the novice Christian had in Rome where he studied at the university from 1971 to 1973 also had a great impact on him. He studied Arabic and Islamic Studies. In those days, he would take turns reading the Bible and reading the Qur'an, in the Arabic language. Together with Claude Rault he founded the group Ribât es-Salâm (Bond of Peace), with the goal of discovering and nurturing the spiritual values that connected both religious traditions in order "to approach God hand in hand." Christian later referred to this as "living in the eyes of God."

Jean-Pierre believes that his desire to get in touch with "the soul of Islam" and to communicate about it with people around him has allowed him to come a long way. Certainly, he never intended to convert to Islam, since he considered himself a Christian once and for all, but he wanted to be as close to his Muslim brothers as he could. Jean-Pierre explains, "He wanted to go to God with them, but with Jesus Christ." He did not aim at "conversion" in the literal sense, but at "creating awareness of God." Jean-Pierre does not deny that this caused numerous conflicts between Christian and his brothers and, of course, also in conversations with his Islamic partners. Nevertheless, all of this did not diminish his attempts to pursue his goal, not even when it posed a threat to his life later, during the Algerian Civil War. Whenever the Prior Christian spoke, his words often reflected a willingness to die.

Jean-Pierre's portrait of **Luc**, the doctor who used to be called Toubib, shows how much he loved this legendary brother of the Atlas monastery. When the thirty-seven-year-old Dr. Dochier became a Trappist monk, he had already served as a staff surgeon in the Moroccan expedition of the French army. In spite of his academic degree, all he wanted was to become a lay brother. From 1943 to 1945, he was a prisoner of war in Wuppertal and voluntarily assumed the role of a family father. As early as in 1959, he had been taken hostage for two weeks for the second time. On the day of the abduction in 1996, he was eighty-two years old and had lived in Algeria for fifty years.

Jean-Pierre mentions numerous details about this boyish guy. Whenever things seemed to turn into a conflict, he was the one who was able to mend the situation. He preferred to wear old and worn-out clothes and shoes made from straw that already had holes. Although he attended Mass daily, he rarely came to the hours of prayer. Because of his asthma and his bouts of coughing, he slept in a sitting position. After he had been abducted, Jean-Pierre found two books on his nightstand, one of which was *Imitation of Christ* by Thomas à Kempis, and a book entitled *Ought We Still Believe in the Resurrection of the Body?* Luc was fascinated with the question of what might happen right after death. His correspondence with other doctors, discovered in a drawer in his room, is evidence for his deeply religious lifestyle and his love for a simple "prayer to Jesus" rooted in the Eastern monastic tradition. He had helped thousands of people in Algeria, and they called him *Marabout* (saint). With respect to his unconventional ways, Jean-Pierre compares him to Saint Philipp Neri, who did not want to be taken seriously.

When Jean-Pierre begins to talk about Toubib and his strange headgear, one right away senses how close he felt to him. Still today he seems to feel brotherly respect for the doctor who had been at work in an abyss of poverty. Comparing the two, one finds out that they are two fundamentally different monks: On one hand Luc, the robust and somewhat unrefined loner who, like an old sailor, loved Edith Piaf's "Non, je ne regrette rien," and on his deathbed he said he would ask for a glass of champagne; on the other hand Jean-Pierre, the faithful and quiet friend who looks at everything with a smile and in a contemplative manner.

Christophe Lebreton was the youngest in the community, and Jean-Pierre had always shown a fatherly kindness to him since he was of an older generation. One could always sense a sort of rebellion in him, but it was usually directed toward himself and helped him to keep track of what was essential in life. On the day of the abduction, Christophe was fifty-six years old and had reached the middle of his life. He was mature and creative and through his presence had a refreshing and encouraging effect on the community of the older monks. Already at the age of twelve, Christophe had entered the "Little Seminary" of candidates for the priesthood, but left it when he graduated from high school in order to study law. He did his civil service in Algeria, and that was to be an omen. After having entered the Trappist Abbey of Tamié in 1971, he moved to Tibhirine when he was still a novice. Six years later, he returned to the Alps of Savoy because he had badly missed them, but in 1990, his search and odyssey ended again in Tiberhine. There he carried out his monastic duties as a gardener, a master for novices, and as cantor. In the garden he worked closely with his Muslim coworkers. In the course of the years, he had only a single novice who later left again, but he had given to him the best part of himself. In the liturgy, he attempted to gradually introduce texts written in the Arabic language and began to include guitar music to accompany the psalms during Easter midnight Mass and at Christmas.

Jean-Pierre says that it was not always easy when in the chapter the different interpretations about reforms and enculturation clashed, and one had to show brotherly patience until a compromise was found that everyone was able to accept. Jean-Pierre with his peasant background and as the son of a miller who had never particularly valued intellectual debates, looked at Christophe and Christian in a contemplative distance when they stuck their heads together in such situations and were far ahead of the rest of the older members of the community in their discussions. This could sometimes also be felt in Christophe's sermons in which he expressed his existential and, at the same time, poetic faith. "It was not always easy to follow him," Jean-Pierre explains with a smile and continues to tell how Christophe had written poems in the silence of his scriptorium that defied any rhyme or rhythm, but always revealed great depth. The poem "The Red Tractor" had particularly impressed him because through simple and familiar images that were taken from the monastic garden landscape, it conveys the rift between fear and hope.

On Christmas Eve of 1993, one of those clashes among the brothers occurred after the "visit" from the GIA, when Christophe was hiding from the rebels in a basin in the cellar and later blamed himself for his "cowardice," because the others had stood up to the danger. Jean-Pierre felt quite close to Christophe and, in those times, did not leave his younger fellow brother alone. "This experience made him more humble and also more loving and helped him develop the willingness to face future adventures of that sort." This attitude is also expressed in one of the hymns that Christophe had composed for the "office of the martyrs." Jean-Pierre had quietly written it down for himself:

Now is the hour of true adoration;
A fire consumes itself in my deepest depths:
It wants to go on to encounter the cross.
Who could defeat this fire?

Jean-Pierre describes his fellow brother **Michel Fleury** as the man of very few words in Tibhirine. Some even saw him almost as a saint. He used to be a milling cutter in an enterprise in Marseille, and in this cultural melting pot had been in contact with Maghrebians early on. He had entered the Abbey Bellefontaine without drawing attention to it, since he loved to live his life in seclusion. Jean-Pierre guesses that it was the death certificate Christian had issued for one of his fellow brothers (Father Aubin) that triggered his decision to move to Tibhirine. The text that moved everyone deeply was about what the presence of Christian monks on Islamic soil signified. Christian depicted this presence as the epitome of personal dedication. Although Michel did not know any Arabic, he still knew Islamic spirituality quite well and always was an active participant of the Ribât encounters that were regularly held and lasted for three days, and from which he would always take home inspiration and incentives.

In Tibhirine, Michel, who loved efficiency and order, worked in the kitchen. According to Jean-Pierre, verbal communication was not one of his strengths; nevertheless, he would often speak up in his striking voice while in the chapter. Jean-Pierre cannot forget one incident that took place the night before Christmas of 1993, when a young GIA combatant led them away and they had to fear for their lives: Michel fully complied and followed the militant without saying a word. Jean-Pierre believed that this was a basic mental attitude that he probably also maintained during his captivity and at his execution.

Bruno Lemarchand is a tragic exception among the seven who were killed. As prior of the small community of Fès, he just wanted to spend a few days in Tibhirine in order to participate in the election of the prior that took place at regular intervals. He departed from Fès on March 18, 1996, determined and disillusioned, because he knew well how dangerous his journey from Morocco to Algeria was. Twenty-four hours later, he arrived at Tibhirine carrying in his luggage several thousand Holy Hosts that had been made in the monastery in Fès. Eight days later when the kidnapping took place, the terrorists did not take into consideration the fact that he belonged to a different monastery, and they deported him, regardless of his protest. Jean-Pierre knew him only superficially, but he was still deeply moved by his assassination, since he later became his successor in Fès. For that reason he tried to find out more about this withdrawn monk who sometimes came across as a bit dismissive. During the clean-up work after the rebels had rummaged through his cell, the documents that were found gave only a few minor hints about his personality. There were only a few letters, some entries in his diary, and a report about his childhood that he had written, it seemed, when he was in his first Abbey of Bellefontaine. It was striking that, similarly to Christophe, Bruno too had been in search of an ultimate monastic home and gone back and forth between Tibhirine and his mother monastery twice during the period between 1984 and 1989.

Similar to the other fellow brothers, Bruno's military service in Algeria played a role for his calling. He felt solidarity with the poor and had an affinity toward the Arabic language. Jean-Pierre thinks his strong character dates back to the time when he taught at Saint Charles College in Thouars. Yet he loved flowers and felt close to the Moroccan gardener, and the two would teach each other Arabic and French. Thami cried bitterly when the news of his death arrived in Fès. Jean-Pierre says about Bruno: "He was a lonely and introverted soul who wanted nothing but to be with God."

Célestin Ringeard wore a copper bangle bracelet around his left wrist; he never said a word about its origin and meaning—it was his secret. Jean-Pierre did not discover a definite explanation for it either when he went through innumerable letters that he had found among his belongings, but he did find information that could be traced back to a marginalized group in society. Before he entered the Abbey of Bellefontaine in the year 1983, the priest had been a social worker and devoted himself to homeless people—alcoholics, drug addicts, and prostitutes. He took care of them and was in contact with them as if they were his own children. And they were so close to his heart that even when he became a monk, he still remained a kind of father figure to them. Many people around him asked themselves the question of how it was possible that such a brilliant and active man became a monk in a contemplative order. Jean-Pierre had answered this question for himself: it was the suicide of a homosexual who one night had called Célestin asking him for help, but upon his arrival, had jumped out of the window—and landed directly in front of Célestin's feet.

His life belonged to those who failed, just like Jesus gave attention to bandits, toll keepers, and prostitutes while being slandered for doing so. Jean-Pierre does not withhold that the extent to which Célestin was involved in these matters, as his correspondence and also his intercessions indicated, was unsettling to the community. Finally they agreed to accept this special and, for a monk, rather peculiar way of pastoral care.

Célestin was an adventurer, and in 1957, he had a similarly shocking experience as Christian de Chergé had had as a young soldier a few years earlier in Algiers when it was shaken by civil war. Célestin, who back then was a paramedic in the French army, once threw himself at the last minute between a friend who was a partisan and the military that wanted to kill him. The partisan had already been shot in his stomach several times with a burst of machine guns, but Célestin was still able to save him. However, until the end, he never disclosed the meaning of the copper bracelet and took it with him in death on May 21, 1996.

For **Paul Favre-Miville**, Jean-Pierre felt particularly deep affection. Both of them came from a rural environment that consisted of simple merchants and craftsmen. Both fully embraced a climate in which faith could be lived freely, a kind of Christianity that focused on work and the life of a priest. Eventually, both of them in their safe worlds experienced a calling to serve God. In 1989 when Paul moved from Tamié to Tibhirine, he right away became friends with everyone. It was quite clear that he was a truly cheerful character. His technical knowledge that he had gained due to being the son of a smith and trained plumber turned out to be indispensable for the work in the garden, the courtyard, the house, and also in his relationship to the neighbors. Even an electrical engineer from Medea asked him for help. Jean-Pierre did like this fellow brother, but for a whole different reason: cheerful Paul always stayed away from chapter meetings when he suspected them of escalating into discussions that could spiral out of control. Although he had his own opinion, he did not share it out of fear that someone might disagree; so he preferred to make his brothers laugh. On one day during such a crisis, when asked how he was doing, he responded with a grin on his face: "My head is still sitting on my shoulders."

Paul thought that Islam had two sides—a spiritual one and a militant one—and although he was familiar with the dangers in Tibhirine, he nevertheless was hard hit by the GIA attack on Christmas Eve of 1993. The situation was so severe for him that the prior had to send him to his sick mother in Savoy. But there his attitude changed like that of Christophe who had once hid in the basement during the first raid, and he wanted to go back. His loyalty to his brothers and to his Algerian friends meant more to him than the safety of his home. Besides, where was his home? Paul took some shovels along on his trip to Algeria. Some people he knew were wondering why, and he told them with a smile in his face: "So we can dig out our graves." Jean-Pierre found it especially tragic that Paul had returned to Tibhirine only the night before the abduction. In a writing of the community there is a sentence that applies to him, the one who had returned home for good, but also to Jean-Pierre, the survivor: "We feel that this trial has changed all of us. One does not approach the limits of violence and hope undisturbed."

July 30, 2011

6:30 AM: Early in the morning when the sun has not yet reached the garden, one has a better understanding of what "maidenhood" means: dew, tender closeness of beauty. Each morning there is another blue and red and yellow color. There is a seamless connection between the tiniest blossoms and the black mountains.

8:00 AM: We are all in love with Baha's apricot jelly. She looks at us with her round eyes and puts her hand on her heart.

8:45 AM: Viola, the Swedish woman, has been waiting for her husband all night long. He arrived with a two-hour delay from Casablanca and is still asleep. She brought along the case with her paintings and looks at me full of expectations. I should hate to disappoint her, and so I say: "There is much love in them."

9:30 AM: In the garden of the monastery I read in the pope's book about Jesus. On every page one can sense the dilemma for this former professor, to keep his theological knowledge in check. In moments when he succeeds, he writes fatherly sentences like these: "Christ Himself as a person is the 'name' of God and makes God approachable to us." [4]

10:30 AM: Jean-Pierre brought me another book: Sheikh Khaled Ben Tounes's *Sufism, the Heart of Islam*. Who could possibly read all of this, dear old friend? He smiles kindly and says, "Only a few pages."

Hedda drags a huge bundle of Lucerne grass on her back to take it to the sheep pen. It is an archaic scene to see a woman as a burden-bearer.

3:15 PM: On the table at the entrance to the guesthouse there is a magazine on display with pictures of the "Holy Mountains." They are memories of my best journeys to various monasteries; they all led eastward: the Skiti Prodromou on Mount Athos, the Cave of Saint John of Patmos, the Hermitage of Makarios in the Egyptian Desert, and now here, Midelt at High Atlas. All of them were journeys to the orient.

---

4 Benedict XVI, *Jesus of Nazareth, Second Part: From Entry to Jerusalem to the Resurrection* (© Libreria Editrice Vaticana: Città del Vaticano; Freiburg im Breisgau: Verlag Herder GmbH, 2011), 110.

5:30 PM: Viola, in her religious zeal, considers missing Sunday Mass as a "capital sin." Jean-Pierre answered her: "Sin is everything that separates us from God. But nobody can escape His mercy." She finds this a strong statement, but wants to think about it more. My friend and poet, the Trappist Charles Dumon, said with a big smile: "We have already been saved. It is all over."

6:45 PM: Jean-Pierre describes a chapter talk that Christian gave in Tibhirine about the "gaze of Jesus." What might it have been during crucial moments—for example, after the betrayal by Peter or the encounter with Judas when he was captured? Artists of all centuries have made efforts to capture the "gaze of the eyes" of the Lord, but even the greatest succeeded only to some extent. Christian added that no one can stop the "trajectory" of this gaze to the Father. Jean-Pierre adds in a whispering voice: "This gaze is irresistible. Whoever is under its spell is moved into a state of conversion."

7:15 PM: For weeks we have been without television or radio broadcasts or newspapers. The only sources for news are the intercessions in the chapel that inform us about an attack in Oslo, the deaths during a crash of a military plane in Morocco, and about the various harvests. We even find out about regional news: a prayer for someone who died in a crash of some sort near Midelt. Lord, hear our prayers. The media is not missed. We get nothing but small glimpses of them; the silence surrounding us amplifies everything.

8:00 PM: As to the question of who had killed the seven brothers, the investigation is still ongoing. Jean-Pierre only knows what has happened inside of the monastery. But the guard reported that one of the kidnappers had said to his companion: "Hurry, get a rope, he will see who we are." They wanted to strangle him, but he succeeded in escaping.

9:15 PM: After Compline: the best hour of the day. The rocks are still hot, but along with the temperature, the tension also decreases. Here one can shake off everything Western and escape one's inner contaminations. The Muslim neighbors wait impatiently for the full moon; soon the fasting month of Ramadan will begin.

·13·

HOTEL BELLEVUE

THE FEAST OF THE VISITATION OF MARY HAS A SPECIAL meaning for the monks of Our Lady of the Atlas. If one reads the texts that the priors of Tibhirine and in Midelt had written on this topic, one could almost assume it was a feast of patronage. When young Mary meets her cousin Elizabeth in Judea, she has a "joyful message" for her. The monks from the Atlas Mountains see themselves on a similarly empathetic mission: they bring to the Muslims their honest beliefs and, in turn, receive a "message" from them that also talks about God. Christian writes: "Our Church does not tell us and also does not know, what the actual connection between our message and the one of the Muslims is. . . . I go to the Muslims, without knowing it."

But then, in one of his writings, Christian describes an encounter that made a deep impression on his old fellow brother Jean-Pierre and has accompanied him throughout his whole life. A deep bond developed between the prior and the Muslim friend after the latter had asked him to teach him how to pray, and for many years there was a lively spiritual exchange between the two. After they had not seen each other for a while due to various other obligations, the Muslim friend said to him, "I think it is time to dig in our common well again." It was an allusion to the depth that characterized their encounters.

Christian responded, "And what will we find at the bottom of the well? Muslim or Christian water?"

Then he looked at him with a mixture of smiling and sorrow: "Do you still ask yourself this question? Don't you know that on the bottom of this fountain we will find the water of God?"

In 1997, when Jean-Pierre was invited to Lourdes on the occasion of a conference of the Reverend Mothers, in order to celebrate Holy Mass with them in the grotto, it turned out to be a very moving experience for him. While he heard the spring water rushing behind him, he talked in his sermon about what Christian had said about this water. "If we dig our well together, we will find God." Jean-Pierre smiles. This is a keen theological observation for someone like him who had never studied theology. "I will never forget this ecumenical theology at the place of the holy water of Mother Mary."

In the months following the abduction and assassination of the seven brothers, a time full of unpredictability, Jean-Pierre twice traveled one thousand kilometers from Fès to Tibhirine. It was a matter of evaluating the situation there, of taking care of a novice from Poland, and of clarifying administrative matters. The community in Morocco comprised only three to four brothers, but it belonged to the monastery Our Lady of Atlas. This small Moroccan monastery that was founded in 1988 and in which Jean-Pierre had an important role to play, dated back to the monks of Tibhirine and, as a spiritual presence, was locally of great importance to the Christian church. Two years earlier, the archbishop of Rabat, Hubert Michon, had visited the monks in Tibhirine in order to gather information about their callings. He was enthusiastic and wished he had a similar community in Morocco, a place that was small and modest, where one lived a life of work while offering a place of silence, primarily to fellow Christians and where one was there for the Muslim neighbors with no intentions of converting them, only offering hospitality.

Christian advised the archbishop back then to turn for help to the Abbot General Ambrosius Southey, as well as to the chair of the Southwest Region of France, Dom Marie-Gérard, and the abbot of La Trappe. Their answer was that this could only be a "branch" of the Atlas Monastery from which only two monks could be taken. Two or three other monks would then come from French monasteries. The proposition was accepted by the majority of the Chapter of Tibhirine on May 25, 1987. "Personnel-wise the decision was not easy," says Jean-Pierre, "but we could not deny the Christians of Morocco permission, especially since the plan was also our ideal.

However, how were things to continue? Jean-Pierre compares the situation with the one in Algeria: the small monastery posed a certain challenge to the order, and one had to ask the question of whether its presence in a mostly Muslim country where one could not expect any "new recruitment" was justified. But he answered the question himself: "We are all engulfed by this Pentecostal spirit that quietly rises from the broken vessel of Tibhirine. It is a secret which we have become part of, a mystery of love that comes from God."

The building in Fès that was found for the community had just enough space for the five residents. It was the former Hotel Bellevue, which the founder of the Little Sisters of Charles de Foucauld, Sister Magdeleine, had acquired in 1954, as a novice. Jean-Pierre describes the house as a place for "hermits that live their lives in a community." It was from the eighth century and located behind the walls of the old part of town, right by the Gate Bab el Did near the Medina, the royal palace, and the Jewish quarter. It had a slightly sloped garden where in the spring gorgeous flowers bloomed. With its lemon and grapefruit trees, as well as two tall palm trees, the place offered an atmosphere that seemed to be taken from the life of Saint Francis.

Nevertheless, Jean-Pierre also noticed disadvantages of the location during his first visit. Unfortunately, the house belonging to the diocese lay somewhat isolated and was surrounded by noise from the street leading to Algeria. Furthermore, the chance to communicate with the local population was limited, and there was a bad smell from all the sewage. On top of all of this, the building was in need of repair. One ceiling had already collapsed, and to restore the house would have been too expensive. There was no workplace except one for making Holy Hosts. Jean-Pierre as acting prior did not see any possibilities to expand the building and set out to search for an alternative place.

In the meantime, his efforts as a survivor from Tibhirine were acknowledged in many European media and church-related institutions. The Belgian newspaper *La Libre Belgique* honored two girls, Julie and Mélissa, who had been murdered, and

Jean-Pierre as a representative of his fellow brothers, and likewise the murdered bishop of Oran, Pierre Claverie, as the "Persons of the Year." Clavier, a Pied-Noir who had sympathized with the independence movement and received Algerian citizenship right after independence had been gained, was a one-time Dominican. The Muslims respectfully referred to him as "Sheikh Claverie." Upon his return from a visit to Tibhirine on August 1, 1996, he died instantly in an explosion late in the evening while entering his home.

The ceremony in the Royal Opera House La Monnaie in Brussels impressed Jean-Pierre deeply. It was a performance of young singers and, as a sign of hope, they showed the image of a bird slowly disappearing. Jean-Pierre was so moved by this that he modified the original text of his speech and talked about the origin of the Rule of St. Benedict of Nursia regarding forgiveness: "We cannot forgive in place of someone else. The founder of an order expects from an abbot to hate that which is not virtuous, but to love the brothers." This trip to Belgium remained an indelible memory for Jean-Pierre. At his reception in the Abbey of Westmalle, Cardinal Godfried Danneels was also present, and during a Mass in the house of the San-Egidio-Society in Antwerp, Jean-Pierre was the one who gave the sermon. In the Abbey of Rochefort he was invited to attend the election of the new abbot. It was Dom Jacques-Emmanuel who was selected and who later moved to Midelt. After his visits to the Trappist convents Nazareth and Soleimont, Jean-Pierre still visited the Abbey of Orval located in the Ardennes.

Nevertheless, he had to find a new home in Morocco. In search of a building suitable to be a monastery, Jean-Pierre came across a house of the former Government of Meknes that in natural surroundings was located halfway to Rabat. Everything looked promising: There was a guesthouse, a small farm, enough rooms, and the salon was suitable to serve as a chapel. Hundreds of olive trees grew on this property consisting of eight hectares, and in the fields there was a water pump. Although the place was quite attractive, there was a problem: foreigners were not allowed to buy land outside of the cities, unless one had "connections," and they did not have any back then.

Finally in 1998, unexpectedly, an offer was made by the Franciscan missionaries of the Mary's Monastery in Midelt, who wanted to give up their house due to their old age. The house was situated two hundred kilometers south of Fès, right in front of the Atlas Mountain Range and not difficult to convert into a contemplative Cistercian monastery. Finally, the search for a new place had ended. It had an alley of pine trees leading to the chapel, and an interior court with a fountain forming the cloister. There was also enough space for guests, and the terraced garden was full of flowers and fruit trees. Finally, the closeness to the city made it easy to have the much desired contact with the locals.

One year earlier, Jean-Pierre had been elected prior by the community in Fès consisting of six people and, therefore, entitled to vote. The presence of the general abbot and the abbot of Aiguebelle underscored the importance of his nomination, and the event signaled a significant change. Fès was now officially the successor of the monastery of Tibhirine, and Jean-Pierre followed in the footsteps of the by now legendary figure Christian. The decision was confirmed by the General Chapter of the Cistercian order in Rome. To the new prior, this meeting, during which he was surrounded by the French and Spanish abbots, was a meaningful experience. "I felt great brotherhood among us," he remembers from this encounter. "We were a universal family."

In March of the Holy Year 2000, the relocation from Fès to Midelt took place. The general vicar of the archbishop of Rabat carried the Mother Mary icon from Tibhirine into the chapel, and Jean-Pierre attached it in the apse while his five fellow brothers followed him. They all hoped for a new beginning, which, however, did not take place at the moment. Dom André Veilleux, his trusted brother from the difficult days of the conflicts in Tibhirine, invited him to Rome, where a gathering of two thousand young people from monastic orders took place. Jean-Pierre sat in the first row and did not know that even the pope would attend. He is almost a little embarrassed about the picture that was taken during the welcome: "It looks as if we embraced each other."

Life in the Trappist monastery of Midelt soon followed the quiet routine of the Cistercian tradition. Some exceptions of the kind the general abbot would permit existed, but other than that, they prayed and worked and had their big and small hourly prayers and the nightly vigil. Together with some young monks, Amédée's attempt to found a new community in Algiers did not materialize. Twice every year, at Christmas and at the feast of Saint Benedict, Amédée visited Midelt because he wanted to show that he belonged to this community. After the attempt to found a new monastery had definitely failed in 2001, he moved to the monastery by the Atlas Mountains. Jean-Pierre says, "Since the death of our fellow brothers, a strong bond had formed between us, but he did not give up the hope of being able to return to Algeria one of these days."

Algeria was still a trauma to him. Bishop Tessier made further efforts to receive permission to make a new beginning in Tibhirine, but it was in vain. He was depressed about it. It was impossible to send out people from the French orders. The Sisters of Bethlehem accepted the invitation of the bishop to live there, but they soon left again. All that was left was the attempt of a "gardener" to retreat to the former gardens of the monastery.

Jean-Pierre looks back at these efforts quite realistically: "The memories are distant; there is a lack of money. Furthermore, the fact that this place is so well known would make it impossible to live a contemplative life. That is not our calling. More and more tourists come to see it, and pilgrims want to visit the graves."

Amédée had settled down quickly in the new Moroccan surroundings. Basically, it was nothing new to him. Jean-Pierre thinks he was made for living together with others. From the beginning, he worked in the laundry and in the electrical workshop. He was no longer a porter as in Tibhirine. His old fellow brother smiles: "Each of us here welcomes everyone. When the phone rings, three people run to the phone."

Then he looks out the window, lost in thought. "Yes, I have grown old, and the road to Timadeuc is far. On the day I entered the monastery, I expected to see the same countryside with its meadows for the rest of my life."

July 30, 2011

6:30 AM: The sun has already reached the yellow walls of the
guesthouse. The petals of the "marvels of Peru" (four-
o'clock flowers) close. They are confidants of the
darkness and its secrets. Flowers whose blossoms
chastely conserve energy during the heat of the day.
They have already said everything there is to say
about the beauty, of which Dostoevsky writes, and
which will liberate us.

7:15 PM: Lauds precede the holy Mass. Psalms about the
joys of life and the spirit of creation are sung.
The Eucharistic Prayer mentions the pope on a
daily basis. It is hard to picture this sophisticated
German correctness in such a tumultuous place
in the foothills of the High Atlas Mountains. If one
reads the pope's book about Jesus, one will find a
great deal of sophistication in it, but also bold
sentences about the afterworld: "Can only that
exist which has always existed? Could there not
be something unexpected, unimaginable, something
new? If there is a God, could He then not also create

a new dimension of human existence or of reality in general?" And further: "Doesn't creation wait for this last and ultimate leap in mutation, for a reunion of the finite and the infinite, the reunion of man and God, a victory over death?"[5]

Jean-Pierre says: "We are standing here in the pull of this boundary."

10:00 AM: Friday prayer of the Muslims, the calls of the muezzins with short breaks in between. In a few days Ramadan, the month of fasting, will begin. The monks of the Atlas monastery participate in it, with the exception of Sundays. The full moon, which is the signal for the beginning of the fasting, is expected to appear the coming Monday at early dawn. Jean-Pierre has passed the age of seventy-five, the age when the rule of the order forbids him to fast. He smiles and says, "I obey."

1:00 PM: Midday heat, a long siesta, nothing moves. There is a feeling of lightness. There is no more poisoning of life through puzzles. Wind and clouds are events

5   Benedict XVI, *Jesus of Nazareth, Second Part: From Entry to Jerusalem to the Resurrection* (© Libreria Editrice Vaticana: Città del Vaticano; Freiburg im Breisgau: Verlag Herder GmbH, 2011), 271.

of the day; bells ringing are the signs of time. Here everyone is equally poor and equally free. Jean-Pierre calls the workers who put water lines in place with Omar or work hard on the garden patches, "models." According to Muslim tradition, the monks and their coworkers greet each other by shaking hands and by saying greetings of peace; there is no ritual, only the joy of life. The community of Midelt is an outpost of the church. More so than in Europe, her members are a Christian minority, but this foreign land is their home. To embrace the simple and small things is their art of living. They do not have big plans, unless it is to preserve a pure heart and, like their seven brothers, to be committed, no matter what might happen.

2:40 PM: In Christian's writings there is a statement about silence from the Desert Father Hyperechios: "The monk says no bad word, because the vine has no thorns."

6:50 PM: When night falls, the bees kiss the four-o'clock flowers awake. But the latter take their time; they have the security of the darkness.

8:00 PM: The pope's words about the beginning of the Last Days continue to have an effect. The ancient Greeks talked about a "veiled image." Paul wrote: "We look as if through a mirror." Ernst Jünger noted, "Maybe it is easier than we think, if it reveals itself within a second."

·14·

THE TESTAMENT

I N THE FORECOURT OF THE ATLAS MONASTERY, HIDDEN BEHIND a brown door with a sign that says "Tibhirine," is the oratory in memory of the seven brothers. The small room resembles a cemetery chapel, but it is a place of hope. Jean-Pierre always enters it with a proud smile on his face, as if he is introducing his family to visitors, and he stands in front of the icon-like portraits of the deceased and does not neglect to point out the picture of Amédée in the lower right corner, who, like himself, had survived the massacre. There is a white area in the lower left-hand corner where Jean-Pierre's picture will be someday—"Whenever it pleases God." He looks forward to this "day of all days."

On the lectern the monks put Christian's last will on display. It is a faithful copy of the original, and one can tell that it has often been gently touched. The text consists of two large pages written in nice handwriting. Although it is a dramatic message from heaven, the handwriting does not indicate in any way that his hand might have been trembling while writing. However, the author had written some words in capital letters and thus given them a special and solemn emphasis among all the other neatly written letters: GIVEN . . . ALGERIANS . . . JOY . . . THANKS . . . GOD-BLESS . . . INCH' ALLAH.

Already now, experts in the field consider this testament to be one of the most important spiritual texts of the twentieth century, as well as a literary document. It was signed on January 1, 1994, and its final draft had been completed on that New Year's Day, a few days after the first assault of the GIA on Christmas Eve of 1993. It included everything that needed to be said. Christian had entrusted the writing that he had put in a double-sealed envelope to his youngest brother, Gérard, in Paris. "Open it, in case something happens," was written on enclosed note.

On the evening of Pentecost in 1996, the time for this had arrived. The news about the assassination of the monks was spreading around the world. When the Chergé family had gathered around his mother, the letter with Christian's last will was opened. The text was so moving that the bereaved family instantly understood that it had gone beyond the scope of the family. Thus they gave the text to the Catholic newspaper *La Croix*, which published it on May 29, 1996. Therein it says:

IF A FAREWELL IS FORESEEABLE

If it should happen one day—and it could be today—, that I become a victim of the terrorism which now seems to be directed against all foreigners living in Algeria, I would like my community, my Church, and my family to remember that my life was GIVEN as a gift to God and to this country. They may assume that the One Master of all life cannot face this brutal way of dying with indifference, and they may pray for me. How can I be worthy of such a sacrifice? May they see this death in the context of so many other deaths that also were results of violence, but that remained unmentioned in these times of indifference.

My life is not worth more than any other, but is also not of lesser value. In no case, however, has it retained the innocence of childhood. I have lived long enough to know that I myself have become an accomplice in the evil which, unfortunately, seems to prevail in this world, even an accomplice of the one who will someday blindly strike me down.

I wish that when the time comes, I will have the clarity of mind that I am able to call upon God's forgiveness and the forgiveness of my brothers and sisters, but also that I can forgive with all my heart the one who is going to slay me.

I cannot wish for such a death, and I feel it is important to admit this. I don't see any reason why I should rejoice that these people whom I love will indiscriminately be accused of having murdered me.

What we may call the "grace of martyrdom" will have too high a price if one blames an Algerian for it, whoever this might be, especially when he claims to act out of loyalty to what he believes to be Islam.

I know full well how much contempt there is for ALGERIANS in general. I am also aware of the caricatures of Islam which have provoked a certain Islamic fundamentalism. It would be too easy to appease one's conscience by equating the religious path of Islam with fundamentalist integralism and its extremists.

I view Algeria and Islam differently: to me they are like body and soul, and I have often enough attested to that. With respect to every-thing I have experienced, I believe that it was right here in Algeria where I have discovered the central theme of the Gospel that I had been

taught on the lap of my mother who was the very first Church I had,
and already back then, I had great respect for Muslim believers.

My death seems to prove those people right who always thought I was
too naïve or too idealistic, and they may say: "Now he should tell us
what he thinks about all of this!" But those who thought so must know
that now, finally, my curiosity is satisfied.

If it pleases God, I will now unite my vision with that of the Father
in order to look with him at HIS children of Islam as He sees them,
fully enlightened by Christ's magnificence, including the fruits of His
suffering, endowed with the gifts of the Spirit, Whose secret joy will
always be to create communion and to restore the similarity while
playing with all the differences among people.

This lost life that is all mine will also be theirs. I thank God, for He
seemed to have created this life as a JOY, against everything and in
spite of everything. This gratitude expresses what has mattered in my
life and certainly also applies to each of you, my friends of the past and
of today, you innumerable dear friends here who stand by my mother's
and my father's side, my sisters and brothers, as it had been promised.

And you, too, are included, friend of my last moment who does not
know what you are doing! Yes, to you, too, I say THANKS and this
GOD-BLESS that you intended. May we see each other again in
Paradise like the fortunate thieves, if it pleases God, the Father of both
of us.

Amen. INCH' ALLAH.
Algiers, December 1, 1993
Tibhirine, January 1, 1994
CHRISTIAN

It is conspicuous that in the small oratory of the "Seven Sleepers" Jean-Pierre not only gently touches the testament of his former prior with his hand, but that he lets it rest there for a moment. This is how people usually revere the relics at a place of pilgrimage. It is a strange and by no means natural touch and points to a development that first led to it. For decades, Jean-Pierre had felt the small rifts in his community, and occasionally he had suffered from them when he sensed discord in the Chapter meetings of Tibhirine. Mostly it concerned questions of lifestyle and the self-identity of the community.

Christian, who as a young priest had lived among artists and students and who had seriously engaged in the study of Islam while he was at the university in Rome, often seemed to be a stranger to the simple fellow brothers in the Algerian Atlas monastery, and sometimes they felt he had ended up at this place by accident. His intellectual abilities and his preference for Islam especially met with resistance from the older monks. Jean-Pierre belonged to this group, and today explains with a smile: "He knew too much." Later he puts it more mildly: "There was a harmony in our diversity."

Only when in the years of threat an entirely different kind of solidarity was needed, the sensitivities ended, because fear was widespread, and there was no longer time to quarrel about theological nuances. Even the elders noticed that their prior was a man willing to accept suffering and was struggling with himself and the existential questions regarding the future of the community. "This is how he was," describes Jean-Pierre, "and since the first attack on Christmas of 1993, we looked up to him. His courage had us convinced."

In the hour of need, all of them moved closer together, and a sense of community was established. All wanted to stay, no matter what would happen. In spite of all the distress, there was hope that was later compared to a burning fire. During the three months after the abduction and all the more after the death notice, this quiet strength took hold of the two survivors. The testament at the deepest level was meant for them because it explained the reasons why they had stayed and revealed a message that hit the core of their calling. Jean-Pierre wrote an impressive commentary on it, not a theological one, but one that was written from his heart and contained everything they had experienced while trembling with fear. The term "A-Dieu" points out the goal, and Jean-Pierre is reminded of the drama of the tragic evening of Maundy Thursday, when "the hour had come." Rarely did I see him that pensive as in the moments when he talked about the death toll that Tibhirine had suffered for this country. To live and to die for Algeria became their only goal in life. Jean-Pierre in his commentary follows the tracks of Christian's testament.

"If a God-Bless is foreseeable"

Already the title of the testament is a summary of its entire content. The word "Adieu" became "A-Dieu" (Toward God). Of course, that was intentional, and it seems to address the following: the moment has come to turn more decisively to God and to more consciously set out on the journey toward this encounter with him. "Toward God" stands more for an attitude that turns its attention to God than for a farewell from this world of people and things that preoccupy us in our daily lives. It is about reflecting upon the path ahead, to look at it and to walk it well. It is the last leg of the journey when everything indicates that the end is imminent. It is the seriousness of existence in which one becomes aware that the hour has come; the seriousness that reminds us of Jesus on the evening of Holy Thursday. In the moment when his Passion begins, Jesus awakes in them a premonition of that which is to come.

"I would like my community, my Church, and my family to remember . . ."

In his message he addresses the people according to how close he was to them, his community, his church, and his family. But which is this "church" that he calls "his church"? He does not say "church," but "my church," and it has a heartfelt connotation: Obviously, he means a bond of love and tender loyalty. Which church did he mean? Presumably, it is the large church of Jesus Christ and the local church of Algiers, which for him becomes an embodiment and takes on a face: this was the place where deep bonds of brotherly love and heartfelt togetherness existed.

"My life was GIVEN as a gift to God and to this country."

It is very important to him that his family would always remember these words because in them lies the essence of his whole existence. That is the meaning of the word "given," which he wrote in capital letters. This self-surrender had a twofold goal: First of all, it was aimed at God to Whom he had dedicated his life through his ordination to priesthood (he had felt this desire ever since he was eight years old). Secondly, it alludes to his calling to live his life in the solitude of the monastery and the decision to live this calling in Algeria. Christian said on All Saints' Day of 1985: "Through the blood of this friend Mohammed who had been killed because he did not want to live a life full of hate, I knew that my calling to follow Christ, sooner or later, needed to be lived in this country because here I had experienced the greatest act of love. I understood right away that this dedication had to result in shared prayers if one wanted to be a true witness of the Church and a symbol of the Community of the Saints."

"They may assume that the One Master of all life cannot face this brutal way of dying with indifference."

How can the only Master and Friend of everything alive allow such a crime? The answer to this question is not simple. However, Christian emphatically invites his family to accept that God is present in all of this, and it is important to look at this idea more closely.

First, there is the expression "the One Master of all life." By using these words Christian refers to a dogmatic formula that has deep roots in the popular belief of Muslims: indeed God is the Master of everything that is alive. Every life lies in his hand, and he deals with it in his wisdom, his power, and his respect for every creature. Nobody has the right to take somebody else's life; God alone decides this. This truth of faith can sometimes help when the sorrow about someone dying is too overwhelming and the trial proves to be too hard. A believer knows that God with his sovereign will wanted it this way and humbly submits to the divine decision like a servant toward his master, who is sure that every decision was made with wisdom.

Christian knew that there was another form of divine presence in our lives. Looking at Christ's Passion and his own life that was connected to the Lord had made him realize that God is very close to those of his children who are in distress.

In a psalm of the Liturgy for Martyrdom it is written: "Precious in the eyes of the Lord is the death of His friends." Christ, in his enduring hope and his defenseless weakness as a true servant of God, his Father, has put himself in the almighty hands of the One and only Master over life. He has resurrected in order to proclaim everywhere that the Spirit, that is the Spirit of resurrection, is stronger than death.

Christian knew very well in whose hands he was putting his life; he had conquered his fear. It was his heartfelt wish to instill in those whom he loved the same outlook on faith, the same trust in the God of love who will not look at this farewell with indifference, but will be united with him.

"May they pray for me."

Many people have eagerly fulfilled this request of Christian. I think of his brothers who experienced the same ordeal, who with him were prisoners in the hands of the abductors for fifty-six days.

What was the content of these brotherly and imploring prayers? Most likely they were praying that they would be steadfast in their beliefs and continue to be loyal to themselves and their old and new tasks, that their charity for all human beings would remain strong and beautiful until the end, whatever might happen; that their hope for the love that is beyond any power may shine as a light in their loneliness; and, finally, that their faith in the mercifulness that is hidden in man be preserved. This also included the belief in the mercifulness of the worst person among them, as the allusion to the "friend of my last moment" indicates. Finally, they prayed that they would be faithful to themselves as monks and, most of all, they implored God to remain in their midst and to keep them together in his mercy.

Christian asked himself, *Who knows if it was not indeed God's will that everything has happened as it did, so that there would be men of prayer among these people of the GIA, monastic men, men who do not return insults when they are slandered, who accept being mistreated silently and without lamenting, who pray and encounter evil with mercifulness and thus leave the path of evil which they, unfortunately, entered, upon seeing these examples of these men of God. How can I be worthy of such a sacrifice?*

"My life has not retained the innocence of childhood."

It is difficult for me to understand why Christian sees himself as an accomplice of evil in this world, he who ever since his early childhood and youth had dedicated his life to God and in the service of others, he who in the last years of his life asked God to turn him into an "unarmed" man hoping that this would also promote the "disarmament" of others—in his neighborhood and in the whole world.

This feeling of complicity with evil, whose fangs extend throughout the whole world—did one have to attribute it in his case to the fact that he felt solidarity with everyone, whoever and wherever they were? Did he want to take the weight of evil that burdens and weakens people upon himself and, as Thérèse of Lisieux phrased it, "sit at the table with the sinners"? In his belief, Christian describes it as "sitting down at the table of the sinners." All of us deserve part of the blame for everything that goes wrong in the family of mankind, and it is our duty to change this and to heal. If we neglect doing this, if we do not take action and carry out the task that we have been given, then we are jointly responsible for the result.

This view of things is not foreign to a monk who feels a calling. He knows that he is an exile, just like Adam was after the Fall, and he strives in his own interest and in the interest of his brothers to rediscover the Promised Land. He feels that he has to work toward reaching this goal in that "School of Charity," his monastery, with everything that is in his power, and he hungers after forgiveness, hungers after forgiving each and every one. He also becomes aware that forgiving is not a matter of wiping out the mistakes, but rather of restoring a broken relationship, healing an injured heart, and not resting until one has reached that goal.

"I wish that when the time comes, I will have the clarity of mind that I am able to call upon God's forgiveness and the forgiveness of my brothers and sisters, but also that I can forgive with all my heart the one who is going to slay me."

"I cannot wish for such a death."

Christian repeatedly said that he did not want to die in an assassination. When someone becomes a martyr, at the same time, someone else bears the blame—and becomes a murderer among brothers. "What we may call the 'grace of martyrdom' will have too high a price," Christian said, especially if the offender were Algerian and acting on behalf of his religion, because through his actions he would also discredit his country and Islam. Christian was always eager to promote religious dialogue. As a result, it was his biggest wish that Christians and Muslims alike would advance by listening to the Word of God and submit themselves to his will. Christian perceived his tragic death that he foresaw not only as a defeat, but also as a major sorrow of the heart.

"I view Algeria and Islam differently: to me they are like body and soul."

Algeria has a lively and rich tradition and a quite peculiar culture. The history of this nation is reflected in certain people and in their faces, in the way they allow a special spirit to enliven them. To Christian it was a world that literally carried him away, a world that he had felt close to for many years. Already during his childhood his curiosity was aroused, and since then the culture and especially the religious life of the Muslims had fascinated him. He wanted to see the spirit that inhabited this culture in action. Moreover, he wanted to feel and touch it. Where did this "spirit" come from, and did it lead to a personal relationship with God? If so, was it possible to travel this path together while supporting each other?

Christian perceived his passionate and brotherly life as a great adventure, an undertaking that corresponded to God's plan for mankind, as he saw it described in the writings and documents of the church: God encounters every human irrespective of the person concerned. Christian followed this idea of walking hand in hand with other "praying people" for part of the way, while being unconditionally faithful to the Christian belief and to his calling as a monk. While doing so he often discovered "a recurring theme of the Gospel," a sign that God's Spirit was at work.

"The central theme of the Gospel that I had been taught on the lap of my mother who was the very first Church . . ."
What wonderful gratitude of a son!

"I was five years old and discovered Algeria during my first stay there that lasted three years. I have always felt great gratitude to my mother for having taught my brothers and me respect for the integrity and the way Muslims pray. 'They are praying,' my mother would say, so I always knew that the God of Islam and the God of Jesus Christ were not different Gods."

Christian had found his true happiness in hearing the heart of this body beating and in gazing into its soul. For this reason he loved to encounter Muslim Sufis and to show everyday hospitality to the common people in the neighborhood, and he also loved to read and think about the Holy Scriptures of Islam.

His mother had conveyed to him a feeling about what it means to be a child of God. Her actions became a lesson of divine wisdom to him, a wisdom that enlightened his mind and accompanied him throughout his life as an inexhaustible source of light and joy. His mother represented the presence of the church, and the child became a bearer of the grace of this church.

HIS children of Islam . . . fully enlightened by Christ's magnificence . . . endowed with the gifts of the Spirit."

The mystery of the Holy Trinity! Christian spelled the word "HIS" in capital letters as an indication of the relationship of the Father to the believers of Islam: they, too, are his children. *HIS*—a word that expresses communion and inexpressible tenderness. Christian wishes to make this perspective his own. He wants to discover the mystery and immerse himself in it in order to be entirely transformed.

"Enlightened by Christ's magnificence!" Is this only a hope for a distant future or does it not already happen here, because the love that has overcome both of these religious communities is already powerfully active and a sign of hope? And did Christ through his Passion not give his life for all of humanity?

"Endowed with the gifts of the Spirit!" Is this possible without having been baptized? One should imagine a city in a "state of occupation," on the brink of capitulation. However in the spirit of God many things look different: behind the city walls there is cheerful complicity. When someone complies after having surrendered, it is not the compliance of a defeated person, but rather it is joy and a shared victory: "Come, Holy Spirit!"

"God seemed to have created this 'lost' life as a JOY. I thank God."

The testament of Christian in which he puts himself, as in his entire life, into the hands of the beloved Lord, can be summarized in one phrase: "Thank you." It is gratitude to a God who, apparently, had created him to experience this joy. And gratitude to the One who had led him in a perfect way to the height of his efforts and who will listen to him and welcome him, a grace that surpasses everything that he could ever have imagined. At the same time, and with the same feeling in his heart, this gratitude also refers to all those who accompanied, understood, and supported him on this sometimes difficult path. It is a heartfelt thank-you to all those companions of hope who worked with him digging an increasingly deeper well of life-giving water, a well shaft full of water that was neither Christian nor Moslem, but simply the water of God.

Through his expression of gratitude Christian shows himself as a profoundly joyful witness to the truth of the Gospel: "[Jesus said,] 'In truth I tell you, there is no one who has left house, brothers, sisters, mother, father, children or land for my sake and for the sake of the gospel who will not receive a hundred times as much, houses, brothers, sisters, mothers, children and land—and persecutions too—now in this present time and, in the world to come, eternal life." (Mark 10:29-30).

"The friend of the last moment"

His last thought belonged to the man who will target and kill him. He calls him the "friend of the last moment." Why? Are these not just words? When he looks at him with kindness here, he does not want to see in him anything but that deep self, a man all on his own, steeped in a hidden thirst for acceptance, welcomed and understood. A man who has rid himself of his sadness and rediscovered the innocence of a child, a true brother in the large family of God's children.

Christian does not want to distinguish between this person and the other Algerians. He wants to open his eyes and his heart to this kind of view that does not make any distinctions between people. Transformed he will resurrect. The love that comes from above is stronger than death—it has to have the final say.

"The One Master of all life cannot face this brutal way of dying with indifference."

Jean-Pierre recognizes in this passage of the testament a strange coincidence, because he knows from thousands of hourly prayers, "how precious in the eyes of the Lord the death of his friends is" (psalm from the litany of the martyrs). He compares them to Christ's crucifixion. The crucified Son of God returns to the merciful God. He sees the pierced fatherly hand. Death, where is your sting? "Christian knew in whose hands he would fall," says Jean-Pierre. "He had conquered his fear."

Sometimes one gets the impression that Jean-Pierre continues to write the testament of his brother, only with different words. In these instances echo and answer subtly touch on each other. When Christian in the beginning of his text asks the community, his church, and his family to pray for him, Jean-Pierre feels the urge to write about the prayers of those who were in captivity for fifty-six days: "What was the content of these brotherly and imploring prayers? Most likely they were praying that they would be steadfast in their beliefs and continue to be loyal to themselves and their old and new tasks, that their charity for all human beings would remain strong and beautiful until the end, whatever might happen; that their hope for the love that is beyond any power may shine as a light in their loneliness and, finally, that their faith in the mercifulness that is hidden in man, be preserved. This also included the belief in the mercifulness of the worst person among them, as the allusion to the 'friend of my last moment' indicates. Finally, they prayed that they would be faithful to themselves as monks and, above all, they implored God to remain in their midst and to keep them all in his mercy."

In 1993, after the political developments in Algeria had spiraled out of control and Christians were murdered in broad daylight, the call for the monks to leave their monastery because it was located in the mountains and thus especially prone to danger became louder. Repeatedly, they rejected this, even when they were blamed for "seeking to die as martyrs." They objected to these kinds of accusations, like Christian did in his testament: "I cannot wish for such a death." To Jean-Pierre, too, it was equivalent to "failing," to die by letting others make themselves guilty. "It is too high a price."

To Christian, Algeria and Islam meant much more than geography and religion. Ever since his childhood he had felt "hints of God" in his life, pointers of which he did not know whether they would lead to his "personal relationship to God." If that, however,

Whenever the brothers celebrate the Eucharist early in the morning, they stand below the old cross of Tibhirine. [below]

The name Tibhirine means "the gardens." They were the workplace of the monks. [below]

Evening fog in Tibhirine; in the nearby mountains there is still snow. [above]

In the deserted interior courtyard all that is left are crosses. The next two pages show the mountains around Tibhirine, the area into which the GIA kidnappers retreated. [below]

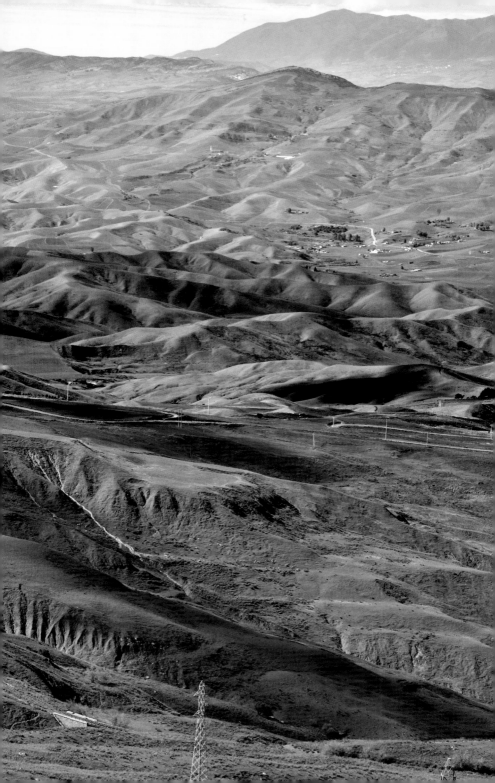

Now and then, a church service is held in the old chapel.

The last survivor
Jean-Pierre says:
"Now all is well."

was the case, he wanted to participate in this "passionate and brotherly adventure."

Jean-Pierre is fascinated by the statement that Madame de Chergé, Christian's mother, had been "the very first Church" to her son, and he points out once more that she was the one who had taught Christian respect for the prayer of Muslims. "They pray" were the words she had given her little son as an answer when he still had no idea about the forms of prayer practiced in Islam.

• Our Lady of Atlas •

August 1, 2011

7:15 AM: Jean-Pierre reads the Gospel about the decapitation of John the Baptist, wearing his bright red robe: King Herod feasting with Herodias, the wife of his brother. Her beautiful daughter dances, and the old man promises her all the kingdoms on earth. His infamous mistress wishes for the head of John. Thus the hangman presents John's head on a plate. The execution of this last prophet weighs more than gold and silver.

The Abbot General Dom Olivera had evoked this biblical scene in the military hospital Ain Naadja, when the coffins that contained the seven heads of the abducted brothers were opened.

The fallen world delights in taking revenge on the saints. The decapitations of the incarcerated John the Baptist and the abducted monks of Tibhirine are connected in a peculiar manner.

7:30 AM: Reading. Dom Olivera writes to all of the four thousand five hundred members of the Trappist order about Christian's "testament," indicating that it represents the overall attitude of the community of Tibhirine.

8:00 AM: Yesterday evening Françoise, the sixty-five-year-old French woman, has arrived from the mountains. For eight days she had supported the Franciscan nuns as an aid worker. Her presence was hidden in the tents that had been set up at an elevation of two thousand five hundred meters where she worked for the seminomadic Berbers: women in labor, children in need, handicapped, ill, and dying people. Without the assistance of charity organizations that send food supplies, medications, and clothing, this operation would be impossible. In former times, she had worked as a manager in graphic design. She was half Jewish, of Polish descent, and had twice survived cancer. After her near-death experiences and the murder of the Trappist monks of Tibhirine, she had radically changed her life. When José is about to serve her food, she is too tired to eat and just takes a big sip from a water bottle. Her clothes are still full of dust, and she yearns to take a shower.

8:45 AM: On a USB stick the prior had saved for me all the
information about the surgeon Elisabeth Lafourcade
who is worshpped in the region of Marabouta (as
a saint). It is his heartfelt wish to make her life
known in Europe: "All these sisters here—each and
every one is a 'Mother Teresa,' yet in silence and
unrecognized."

Jean-Pierre reasserts that the relationship
between monks and women in the Atlas monastery
was straightforward and without difficulties.
Decades earlier, he had witnessed a quite different
and tense situation behind the walls of Trappist
abbeys: "I give thanks in front of the icon of Mary
that this has been overcome."

My objection that the Bible contains only few
references to Mary, just a few verses in Isaiah and
some in the New Testament, he answers again with
a gentle smile: "I believe Mother Mary speaks for
herself, especially this mother."

12:10 PM: Jean-Pierre repeatedly mentions his cranky friend
Luc: "He was old and asthmatic. What might he have
experienced during the fifty-six days of abduction?
Earlier, we had to put on Edith Piaf when he was

ill. His favorite book in the Bible was the book Koheleth and the verses about the thieves. They are exclusively stories that have to do with death. After his death we read the letters to his friends, and each of them was a treasure: "An ill person is neither a soldier nor a resistance fighter, but a person in need. We don't check his identification. The oath that we have taken as doctors obliges us to take care of all sick, even the devil."

When Jean-Pierre was overcome by doubts and he confided in Luc, the latter would put his arm around his shoulder and say: "You know, in face of so much violence, there are only two options, to either act like Maximilian Kolbe and 'become a substitute,' or 'to suffer along' like Jesus did."

3:30 PM: Jean-Pierre is asked whether he can imagine that one had discovered the heads of the brothers in a tree on the road to Medea. He looks at these macabre things with a sober mind: "They just wanted to prove that my fellow brothers were really killed by terrorists. Maybe it would also have been too difficult to transport their bodies through the mountainous territory." He knows the place quite well: "It was a tree in the outskirts of the city, close to the gas station."

5:00 PM: Jean-Pierre is once again asked for his advice. Pretty often it concerns death and the devil, and above all the older people are afraid, but he does not share their fear: "Cardinal sins are committed far more rarely than we think. The devil only triumphs when someone intentionally commits evil. His goal is to separate man from the vital stream of life. He is the big divider."

8:00 PM: Silence, hardly any wind in the trees. The bell rings for Compline, the nightly and farewell prayer. I will take all of this with me back to Europe. Just now we talked again about death, and Jean-Pierre smiles like a little boy: "I hope this very much longed for encounter will be a feast. One has to be prepared for it. I pray to our Lord every night that he prepare me, and I also turn to His Holy Mother that it may become the most beautiful day of my life."

RED CARPET FOR TIBHIRINE

WORK ON THE PRODUCTION OF THE MOVIE *OF GODS and Men* were days of happiness for the actors, the producer, and the film director alike. When on May 18, 2010, it was first released at the International Film Festival in Cannes, the official showing was followed by applause that lasted for ten minutes, and the media celebrated the film. One week later, the jury awarded the movie a Grand Prix, and the actors, producer, and film director saw themselves on the red carpet of the festival hall, surprised, somewhat shy, smiling as if they could not quite believe that this was happening. Most of them wore tuxedos; Sabrina Ouazani, who played Rabbia, the young girl from Tibhirine, a long flame-red dress. Next to her, as in the movie, was Michel Lonsdale, unmistakably Toubib Luc, in a white jacket and a red scarf. Lambert Wilson, who played Christian, was there with sunglasses, far taller than all the others. If one is familiar with this humble and dramatic movie, it is almost a surrealistic sight, but the response of the audience proved the jury's decision right. Worldwide millions of people watched the film, and soon it came out as a DVD. Great cinematic art had caught up with the glamour of Cannes, as had the viewing public at large.

In April of 2006, the producer, Etienne Comar, had seen the documentary *The Testament of Tibhirine* by Emmanuel Audrain and was deeply impressed. In 2007, he suggested making a movie of it to the film director Xavier Beauvois. He knew that the latter was always looking for strong characters and powerful themes, and during the production tended to stay in the background, as if he were working on a documentary. Together they wrote the screenplay that centered on the depiction of the monks who were determined to stay in Algeria at any cost. It was an ambitious endeavor, but they tried to let the writings of Prior Christian and the poet-monk Christophe inspire them in order to get as close to the events as possible.

Before the film production started, the actors spent a week in the Trappist Tamié Abbey. They lived in the barren cells of the monastery and also practiced singing Gregorian and liturgical songs. Henry Quinson, the author of the book about Tibhirine and formerly a monk in Tamié, gave advice to the whole crew about sound, backdrops, and costumes that would be true to the strict lifestyle of Trappist monks. Finally, the screenplay was shown to the families of the victims and the monks of Tamié, where it provoked numerous objections. For security reasons, using the deserted monastery of Tibhirine that was originally chosen as the location for the production was out of the question. So it was decided that it should be produced in Morocco instead, in Toumliline, where at an elevation of 1,600 meters a former Benedictine monastery was located. Most of the critics of the project feared reprisals for the monks of Midelt. Apparently, the advisor Quinson had nightmares: "I am the gravedigger of Midelt."

It is important to mention that the somewhat strange title *Of Gods and Men* had been clear from the beginning and that Beauvois could not be talked out of it. It referred to Psalm 82, verses 6 and 7 in the Old Testament where it says: "I said, 'You are gods, sons of the Most High, all of you; nevertheless, like men you shall die, and fall like any prince."

However, the movie does not show the actual killing of the monks, neither are the horrible crimes associated with the Algerian Civil War further discussed. On the contrary, at the center of the film is the Rule of Saint Benedict: "*Ora et labora—* pray and work." The terrorism is only depicted as evil in local and regional respects. The true battle is fought within the hearts of the individuals and centers on their free decision in view of a danger that could result in their deaths, until the focus is increasingly put on the question of martyrdom. The term, which is generally avoided in the film, only appears in a quote from Christian's testament: "What we may call the 'mercy of martyrdom' will have too high a price if one blames an Algerian for it, whoever this might be."

As a result, nearly imperceptibly, the tragic theme of the self-sacrifice becomes the focus of the plot, and almost an atmosphere of antiquity prevails throughout the rest of the movie: one of the last scenes shows images that evoke the Last Supper on Holy Thursday. The monks are gathered in the Chapter Hall while Luc plays a tape with Tchaikovsky's "Dance of the Swans," reflecting the powerful and strong emotions before a tragic farewell that takes place in snow and fog.

During the production—when they were filming the abduction and had just blasted a door to the monastery—it suddenly began to snow, which caused Xavier Beauvois to spontaneously change his original plan of showing the murder of the monks. Instead he chose the image of a group, consisting of monks and abductors, slowly disappearing in the fog and vanishing into the mountains. Jean-Pierre says, "What stays with the viewer is an image of the unknown. . . . It is a beautiful mystery at the peak of their dedication to the Lord and the Algerian people."

In view of his own late phase in life, this film is unexpectedly important to Jean-Pierre since, by the means of art, as through a mirror, he approaches the mystery of the seven brothers. To the images that this old man already holds in his heart new ones were added, but not different ones, and a message of "hope against all hope" was spread all over the world. The last survivor of Tibhirine is not alone. He senses the solidarity of millions of people, even of those who don't have much faith. "This film moves me," he says in a quivering voice, and if he were to say more he would cry.

Jean-Pierre does not deny that at first he and his brothers in Midelt had rejected the film project. "We were against producing the film in Morocco because we did not want anyone to suspect we might be out to proselytize and try to convert Muslims to Christianity. That has never been our intention. Already in Tibhirine this was completely out of the question for us. One should never forget that we lived quite reclusive lives. At the time the project was planned, some people were still denied an immigration visa. One claimed it was for security reasons." The second reason why the monks were hesitant about the film project is understandable as well: "We feared the movie might not live up to accurately representing the true testament of the brothers and their fate. However, when the production had begun, we quickly learned that our fears were unfounded. I hope people understand these concerns. I am a little ashamed that I am suddenly well-known. We monks live reclusive lives."

The depiction of the relationship between the monks and the local population also had to be done sensitively and diligently. It was important to find the right tone and subtle imagery. In this context Jean-Pierre remembers the year 1964, his first year in Tibhirine, when immediately after Algeria had gained independence, xenophobia caused attacks on anything that was reminiscent of the country's colonial past. At the time, the monks decided that if they ventured out of the monastery, they would only dress as civilians. Jean-Pierre smiles because he thinks about one exception: his beloved friend Luc continued to tend to the sick in his brown monk habit that resembled a Djellaba. His reason for this was: "I am not afraid of death; I am a free human being."

In spite of all the objections that were made against the project, the film producers did not want to accept them, because they knew what they wanted: they were not looking for glamour or action, but for deep empathy. In retrospect Jean-Pierre says, "They were quite respectful. Their respectfulness is also reflected in the wonderful authenticity of the film, even though some of the details do not correspond to what actually happened. For example, my brother Amédée would have never hidden underneath his bed out of fear during the night of the abduction. He was known to be sensitive and endearing, but he was not at all an easily frightened person."

Jean-Pierre does not agree with the critical comments that were made about the part of Prior Christian that was played by Lambert Wilson, who apparently came across as too harsh and too brooding. Rather, he points out that one has to consider the dangerous situation that the community was in: "He was no longer the cheerful Christian of the carefree years. I admire him in this part, for how he listens to the brothers, especially in the difficult moments. He does not want to impose anything on them and strives to seek God. Through this he shows a behavior that is typical for a monk." Jean-Pierre refers once more to the testament that was written three years earlier and was the result of a strong passion: "In the months of the increasingly dreadful trial, this passion had to prove itself, and he had to prove it to us, his brothers, without leaving any doubts. His example was fantastic. Our decision to stay with the poor people of Tibhirine was unanimous."

Jean-Pierre is overjoyed by the thoroughness with which the actors had prepared themselves for their parts. He right away recognizes himself in Loïc Pichon, who played his part, "although we are not at all alike." Later he wrote him the following note: "All of you succeeded to immerse yourselves in the souls of the monks. . . . How beautiful, how wonderful!" Jean-Pierre is happy about the efforts that were made in the Tamié Abbey to learn about the everyday life of Trappist monks: "The actors underwent a transformation of themselves and tried to be true to the mystical reality. They even learned to sing Gregorian songs. I think they sang even better than we."

The film shots that depict even minute details of the quiet landscape show that all that matters is what Jean-Pierre calls "the message." "The movie is an icon, that is, it contains more than what it shows. . . . The Gregorian songs, they are more than musical notes; they touch something deep inside of us. This film is a masterpiece."

On November 4, 2010, something special happened in Rome. The movie *Of Gods and Men* was shown to the plenary meeting of all male and female prior generals. Afterward the abbot emeritus of the Belgian Trappist Abbey of Westmalle, Dom Yvo Dujardin, gave a speech. It was a risk to add a talk to a movie that had already lasted two hours. Some of us would just like to retreat into a remote room, said the monk who admits that he had cried when he heard about the deaths of the monks of Tibhirine. But he felt he had to put the killings in the broader context of the Algerian Church that recorded seventeen deadly attacks between 1994 and 1996.

In contrast to the other twelve victims who were assassinated in the end of 1993, after they had been asked to leave the country, the monks in Tibhirine had been warned by the terrorists that they would come back. Dom Dujardin senses in this a special calling, to illustrate "the inner fire of all the other people in Algeria," and he explicitly recognizes this fire in the dead as well as in the survivors. By the latter he explicitly refers to Amédée and Jean-Pierre. He continues that they, too, have the task to tell the story of the slain brothers and sisters. In his view, through Tibhirine, the charisma of the Cistercians has received a new "symbol of missionary presence in the world"—no matter whether one lives one's belief in danger or in peace, and the film gives expression to this symbol.

Henry Quinson, the "monastic advisor," dedicated a book to the spiritual background of the movie and wonders why it was such a worldwide success: "Was it the people who made the movie possible? The small monastery that was lost in Algeria has turned into a 'miraculous social phenomenon.' Does it hold a deeper secret?" Film director Xavier Beauvois expressed it even more clearly before the film was produced: "I want to show the secret of the incarnation in the Eastern world." Considered to be a disbeliever, he admits: "I have fallen in love with these monks, and the only way I can capture and convey this is by using light. We will let the light of these brothers shine throughout the whole world like stars in the sky."

August 2, 2011

8:30 AM: When one packs one's things together after weeks in
a monastery, the objects assume a spiritual gravity.
The notebooks are filled with records of intense
conversations. The Book of Hours contain the small,
seemingly unimportant events of a certain day or
night. The ink in my ballpoint pen is almost gone,
and there are bookmarks in the books written by
the pope and Ernst Jünger. The alarm clock is set
for 3:45 AM, the time for the nightly office. Beneath
the star-filled sky a flashlight was not necessary.
The flower seeds were wrapped up like drug powder.
Before my departure the prior still gave me a USB
stick with the important documents. Even my
toothbrush has a different meaning; it is a sign of
the beginning of richer days.

I read as much and as often as I could in the books
and writings that Jean-Pierre had given me and
organized the loose notes. They are all important
passages and documents of a certain presence in
seclusion. Some of the words written by Luc to his

nephew in Paris were underlined in red: "I am old, sick, and tired. Man is only a miserable thing if his soul does not sing. I ask the Lord to grant me joy."

9:00 AM: One last look at the countryside, the garden arranged in cascades, and the fruit trees; the four-o'clock flowers, which only close at first dawn, the mallows bending in the gentle wind, and the roses. Behind this the peak of the High Atlas Mountain, powerful and quiet like God's Mountains in the Bible.

9:40 AM: The chapel is still empty, only Jean-Pierre appears once in a while from the sacristy and prepares the altar table. This is the focal point of all things, the place of long prayers on day and at night, the place of the Eternal Light, the cross and the icons whose golden gleam sets itself apart from the plain stone of the walls. All of this radiates something symbolical, the harshness of the desert, and the treasure in the field.

The gate only consists of a large mosquito screen, and the heat comes in as if there were a hidden fire glowing inside.

10:00 AM: Sunday Mass before my departure where I see everyone again: my fatherly companion Jean-Pierre, slightly bent with the smile of a heart that is at peace; the prior, casual and self-assured; José-Luis, the most cheerful of all; and the lean Godefroid focused on playing the zither; then the line of sisters dressed in light summer outfits and immersed in prayers. A woman from Korea does the reading. Finally, in the last row, there are my three Spanish friends, freshly showered, as if they were standing guard.

11:15 AM: In the chapel of Charles de Foucauld, which I had entered right upon my arrival. Empty churches radiate a strong divine presence. Great silence around the Saint of the Desert. He stands for the beginning of a new orientation of the church toward Islam. Prayer in the language of solitude, love for others that does not ask for anything in return, humble search after a shared Father. Blood as seed for the spirit. Christian spent a time of crisis in the hermitage of the "little brothers" in the Hoggar Mountains. Jean-Pierre says: "He returned a changed man."

1:15 PM: At the table, conversations about the success of
the film by Xavier Beauvois. Comparisons with the
grain seed, the mustard seed. Through the cross
to the light. Even prior to the prize ceremony, the
world press in Cannes enthusiastically received the
film, with some viewers crying. In the chaos of the
time, the film offered a moment of light, in the global
turmoil a sign of silence; for two hours a feeling of
healing prevailed because there was someone who
had dared to speak of God again.

2:00 PM: The embraces of farewell. To leave people with whom
one has become familiar is a little bit like dying.
The four monks are standing in the glowing sun.
Wholehearted goodness, shiny eyes, waving hands.
Jean-Pierre, the shortest and oldest among them.
Probably we will never see each other again, but
everything will be preserved in our hearts. Then the
large wooden gate opens. Dust rises. Adieu, Midelt.
Adieu, good friend.

ABOUT THE TRAPPISTS

THE MONASTIC ORDER OF THE TRAPPISTS IS THE RESULT OF several reform movements. It originated in the twelfth century in the French Abbey Cîteaux (Burgundy). Rooted in the Benedictine order, the new branch spread all over Europe under the influence of Bernard of Clairvaux. After its demise in the sixteenth and seventeenth centuries, the order whose monks called themselves Cistercians was reformed again, especially in 1662, under the guidance of Abbot Armand Jean de Rancé in the Abbey La Trappe (Normandy), from which the "Trappists" took their name. In the Catholic Church the order has had the name "Cistercians of the Strict Observance" (O.C.S.O.) since 1903.

The reform of La Trappe was characterized by a strict life of prayer and work, silence, nightly wakes, and asceticism. The spiritual life of the order draws on the Bible, the Rule of St. Benedict of Nursia, as well as mystical writings of the early monks and Desert Fathers. Trappist cloisters usually are located in remote areas and are characterized by simplicity. The monastery currently has one hundred and two communities worldwide with 2,083 members. The seventy-four convents have altogether 1,735 sisters (as of 12/2010).

In Germany, in the Eifel area, there are Trappist monasteries in Mariawald and in Maria Frieden (women); the Austrian Trappist monks live in Engelszell. The members of the order wear a white habit with a black scapular and leather belt and, as choir habit, the white monk cowl. The most famous among them, later in the twentieth century, were the Sahara hermit Charles Foucauld, the American writer Thomas Merton, as well as the prior of the Algerian monastery Tibhirine, Christian de Chergé.

Further information at www.ocso.org

ABOUT THE AUTHOR
Freddy Derwahl

Born in 1946 in Eupen, Belgium, he studied literature and sociology in Leuven, Aachen, and Paris. He was a journalist and reporter for a German daily newspaper in Brussels, later editorial journalist at the BRF, the Belgian broadcast and television station (among other things, as director for the BRF cultural program). He spent a sabbatical in the USA and was a guest auditor at the Lateran-University in Rome. Since 2007, he has been a freelance writer. He is also a member of the PEN Club.

In the German-speaking world, he became known through his publications about Pope Benedict XVI, "the one who came on a bike and in an Alfa," as well as his biography about Father Anselm Grün. Further publications appeared in the German newspaper *Die Zeit* and the ARTE and ORF TV stations.

As a young man he was a candidate (postulant) in the monastery of Tibhirine and, therefore, knew the monks that were murdered. Jean-Pierre, the last survivor of the massacre, is a father-like friend to him.

THE PHOTOGRAPHER
Bruno Zanzoterra

Born in 1957 in Monza, Italy, Zanzoterra as a youth had great interest in Celtic culture. His first reports were about the Dublin of James Joyce and the Vikings on the Shetland Islands. In his old

Peugeot 404, he undertook his first trip from France to Africa, from the Sahara desert to the Atlantic coast, and to the states in the Gulf of Guinea at the end of 1979. Since then he frequently spent time on the Black Continent. He repeatedly did photo reportages about African countries and their peoples. He is the cofounder of the Agency "ParalleloZero" in Milan, Italy, and contributor to numerous geographical and travel magazines, among them *Geo, Focus, Figaro-Magazine, Airone,* and *Panorama Travel.*

ABOUT PARACLETE PRESS

Who We Are

Paraclete Press is a publisher of books, recordings, and DVDs on Christian spirituality. Our publishing represents a full expression of Christian belief and practice—from Catholic to Evangelical, from Protestant to Orthodox.

We are the publishing arm of the Community of Jesus, an ecumenical monastic community in the Benedictine tradition. As such, we are uniquely positioned in the marketplace without connection to a large corporation and with informal relationships to many branches and denominations of faith.

What We Are Doing

Books | Paraclete publishes books that show the richness and depth of what it means to be Christian. Although Benedictine spirituality is at the heart of all that we do, we publish books that reflect the Christian experience across many cultures, time periods, and houses of worship. We publish books that nourish the vibrant life of the church and its people—books about spiritual practice, formation, history, ideas, and customs.

We have several different series, including the best-selling Paraclete Essentials and Paraclete Giants series of classic texts in contemporary English; Voices from the Monastery—men and women monastics writing about living a spiritual life today; award-winning poetry; best-selling gift books for children on the occasions of baptism and first communion; and the Active Prayer Series that brings creativity and liveliness to any life of prayer.

Recordings | From Gregorian chant to contemporary American choral works, our music recordings celebrate sacred choral music through the centuries. Paraclete distributes the recordings of the internationally acclaimed choir Gloriæ Dei Cantores, praised for their "rapt and fathomless spiritual intensity" by *American Record Guide,* and the Gloriæ Dei Cantores Schola, which specializes in the study and performance of Gregorian chant. Paraclete is also the exclusive North American distributor of the recordings of the Monastic Choir of St. Peter's Abbey in Solesmes, France, long considered to be a leading authority on Gregorian chant.

Videos | Our videos offer spiritual help, healing, and biblical guidance for life issues: grief and loss, marriage, forgiveness, anger management, facing death, and spiritual formation.

Learn more about us at our website: www.paracletepress.com, or call us toll-free at 1-800-451-5006.

SCAN TO READ MORE

You may also be interested in

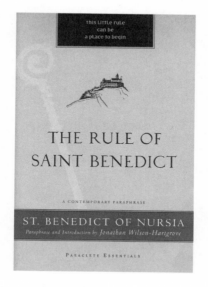

The Rule of Saint Benedict

Paraphrase and Introduction by
Jonathan Wilson-Hartgrove

ISBN: 978-1-55725-973-8 • $13.99 Paperback

THE ENTIRE TEXT OF THE *RULE* IS HERE, PLUS A LENGTHY introduction from Jonathan Wilson-Hartgrove. Detailed explanatory notes throughout explain difficult passages. The result is a classic reintroduced that will enliven any twenty-first-century expression of religious community.

The Rule of Taizé
French and English Translation

ISBN: 978-1-61261-305-5 • $16.99 Paperback w/ French Flaps

THE STORY OF TAIZÉ IS WELL-KNOWN. MORE THAN FIVE MILLION people—particularly the young—have pilgrimaged there to pray, study the Bible, and discover the fruits of living and working beside other Christians. After Brother Roger's untimely death in August 2005, the Community republished *The Rule* in French and prepared a fresh translation into English. This work of deep insight and broad vision is a mine of wisdom for all those seeking to live in harmony with others and with God.

Available from most booksellers or through Paraclete Press:
www.paracletepress.com • 1-800-451-5006
Try your local bookstore first.